Thank you for purchasing *If Only I Had a Place*. This guide will give you both standard and "inside" information on how to secure the best places to live in Mexico for the least cost. It also has a listing of rental concierges - real people who can preview any place you're considering, along with tips on how to make your first long-term stay count the most in planning your life in Mexico, whether full or part-time.

Go to www.ventanasmexico.com and the *If Only I Had a Place* book blog for additions and changes to the rental concierge listing and book updates. The website and regular blog provide valuable insights and advice on living in Mexico.

If Only I Had a Place

What Every Potential Expat Needs to Know About
Renting Well in Mexico

(Listing of Rental Concierges Included)

Dedicated to Elise Page, my friend,
business associate and Mexican fast track.

Table of Contents

Introduction

Over 300,000 people in the U.S. say that they are seriously considering permanently retiring to Mexico. Many see living in Mexico as a viable, sensible alternative to the high premiums and at times outrageous drug costs associated with the U.S. healthcare system. These lower medical expenses and Mexico's overall lower cost of living is reviving in some the dream of a comfortable retirement.

Others are considering living in Mexico part-time or temporarily to test the waters, perhaps doing remote work in a country where the daily level of stress is lower and the daily news arguably more "*amena*," especially of late.

Every single one of these aspiring expats will need to visit the country first. Each will need to determine the kind of city they want to live in and the style of housing they like and can afford. All need to get a feel of what it's like to live where another language is spoken before making a longer-term commitment.

If you are one of these people, and I assume you are if you are reading this book, your first stays in Mexico will be pivotal to your decision on whether to become a full- or part-time expat, either catapulting you towards an exciting new life phase or closing the door on what might have been.

Where you live and your experience while renting the first few years will form the basis of what you believe about Mexico and Mexicans. This isn't a book about just "finding a place." It's about developing a *system* that will serve you year after year, for either the first few years while deciding upon permanent residency or one you can employ in order to live in Mexico part-time indefinitely.

This book is not written for people trying to live on $1,000 a month in Mexico. For one thing, the current income requirement for a "Visa Temporal" is $2,500 a month or proof of assets of over $99,500 (The amount seems to vary from state to state).

Many people who have always considered Mexico their "last resort" are now learning that the door to retire in Mexico on social security alone has closed - at least it has if you're intending to do it legally.

A regular tourist visa allows you to stay 180 days. You may seek a temporary visa to stay up to a year. Probably the best thing to do is apply for your "Visa Temporal," before you leave the U.S., for the first stay since it requires you to travel to Mexico within 180 days and make several trips to the Immigration office while you are there.

The application only costs $36. You do need to show proof of income or assets along with filling out an application and providing two pictures. Why not get the ball rolling?

Having a person "on the ground" in Mexico - Rental Concierges

For most people, one of the scariest things about planning a long-term stay in Mexico is renting a place, especially if trying to do so from a distance. Lack of familiarity with neighborhoods and regulatory protections in Mexico can provoke a great deal of anxiety.

For me, having someone "on the ground" has been crucial to my peace of mind. In my particular case, taxes and work bring me back to the States for at least a month a two a year.

Every time I prepare to go back and rent a new place (I like to try different neighborhoods), my rental concierge inspects the one or two that have made it to my short list. She takes pictures and notes of intangible qualities like coziness and neighborhood ambience.

This experience inspired my efforts to scour Mexico for people who could serve this same function for other expats. I'm really proud to represent them in this book. Although each rental concierge is unique, they all share key characteristics:

<u>Familiarity with their area:</u> Whether an expat or bilingual Mexican national, each person listed knows their town intimately and will be able to fill you in on its unique qualities and life in Mexico.

<u>Online Presence:</u> All have some type of online presence, either through blogs, business Facebook pages, business websites or a long history of doing business in their

city as realtors or property managers. Many were referred to me by expats who have spent years in their given town.

Enthusiasm for their city: I'd hate to be hosting a cocktail party for all of them at once because I'm sure it would end up in a fist-fight over who lived in the best city in Mexico.

All of them can provide a wealth of information about your target Mexican city (once you hire them of course).

Synopses of Favorite Expat Cities and Rental Concierge Information

Chapala

With some of the best weather in the world, Chapala, along with Ajijic, are expat havens, having all the comforts and services of an American city. Nearby Guadalajara (Mexico's second largest city) has excellent medical care and an international airport. Lake Chapala is Mexico's largest freshwater lake so like big lakes everywhere, the area attracts week-end recreational users. In this case from nearby Guadalajara, although in the last few years, the shallow lake has had some pollution issues.

Some top end expat community developments are Arroyos, Chula Vista North, El Palmar Courtyard, Lomas de Ajijic, Rancho de Oro, Riviera Alta and Villa Nova. Lake Chapala has a large foreign community, estimated at 40,000 if you include snowbirds and permanent residents. The city boasts over 50 organizations to support its foreign community. In addition to the Lake Chapala Society, they have American Legion, the Canadian Club, a French group, German group and Irish and British Societies.

Ajijic - also along Lake Chapala, is probably the area most supportive of expats in all of Mexico. Around 5,000 expats live there. The wonderful climate makes it possible to enjoy tennis, cycling, hiking, golf, horseback riding, swimming. You name it and the facilities are available.

The extremely active Lake Chapala Society, which serves both communities, hosts numerous events, organizes volunteer opportunities, gives advice on health services available to expats and offers an extensive English-language library.

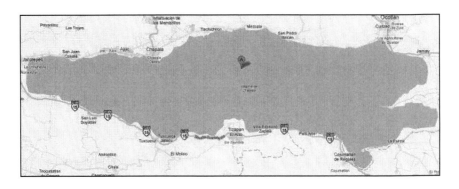

Ajijic and Chapala are along the southern shore of the lake. - [Google maps]

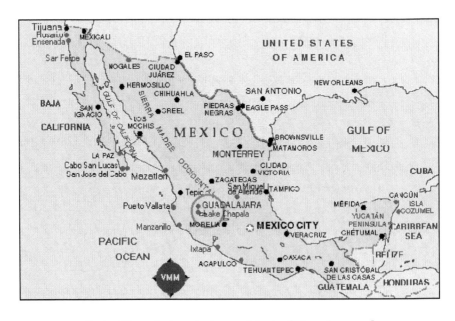

Lake Chapala in relation to Mexico [Google maps]

<u>Weather</u>: The year-round average temperature is about 72 °F (22). It is seldom too hot or humid. The rainy season goes from June to October with an average rainfall of approximately 34 inches and generally occurs during the evening or at night.

A recommended rental websites: www.chapala-pa.com, *Guadalajara Reporter* and *Oro del Lago*

Rental concierges for Lake Chapala/Ajijic area: Judy Dykstra and Audrey Zikmund

Judy Dykstra
Lake Chapala
E-mail: Jubob2@hotmail.com
Jubob2 - Skype
Website/blog: judykystrabrown.com
387-761 0281

What Judy loves about Lake Chapala: "I moved to San Juan Cosala, near Ajijic, Jalisco, Mexico in 2001 and have never once regretted it. A great many expats have moved here since then but It remains Mexico. We love the difference that the mañana philosophy and the emphasis on family life over business imparts to our lives"

Judy's book of poetry, Prairie Moths: Memories of a Farmer's Daughter (nonfiction/memoir), Lessons from a Grief Diary: Reinventing Your Life after the Death of a Loved One, and her children's picture book Sock Talk are available on Amazon and Kindle. She's also working on two more books and posts daily on her blog at judydykstrabrown.com

Audrey Zikmund
Lake Chapala
E-mail: az62343@gmail.com
Home: 376-106-0821
Cell: 331-862-7148

What Audrey loves about Lake Chapala: "The people in Lake Chapala are friendly and it doesn't take long to get involved in many, many volunteer projects available serving the local community or things that you have been wanting to do but never got around to. This truly is a place for all seasons, not talking about the weather but about the seasons of our lives."

Guadalajara

Guadalajara is Mexico's second largest city (over four million people) enabling it to offer the excitement of any diverse cosmopolitan center along with Mexico's traditional colonial plazas, city squares, and parks. More than a tourist area, Guadalajara is a commercial center, Mexico's "Silicon Valley" - attracting Mexico's brightest and most ambitious.

The estimated 50,000 expats who make Guadalajara home are absorbed into the city rather than concentrated in any given neighborhood. In fact, the city lacks a distinct expat community, causing many expats to elect to live in nearby Lake Chapala about 45 minutes away. Tlaquepaque, a city about six miles outside Guadalajara, so far is the closest to having traction as an expat area.

Expats can keep in touch with one another in Guadalajara (if they elect to do so) through the American Society of Jalisco (the Mexican state in which Guadalajara is located). Meetups (through Meetup.com) are another popular way to meet expats and locals through gatherings based on shared interests, like photography or yoga. The English-language *Guadalajara Reporter* has long served the expat community there.

Guadalajara has a large city's typical penchant for overwhelming nightlife, a culture that includes several dance and ballet companies, and a shopper's paradise. Among the numerous malls is the largest in Latin America, with 220 stores.

The Libertad Market is the largest outdoor market in the hemisphere. Large-scale events such as the Guadalajara International Film Festival, and the Guadalajara International Book Fair draws international crowds to Guadalajara. The price for these large city benefits is made payable in a higher level of pollution and more petty crime common to such large cities.

Guadalajara International Airport serves the city and surrounding regions. The city itself has excellent public transportation. Expats from Lake Chapala and even Puerto Vallarta (four hours away) come to Guadalajara for their major healthcare needs as many doctors in the city are U.S.- trained.yM

<u>Weather</u>: Guadalajara has a reputation of being the city of perpetual spring, with cool, fresh mornings, days that usually stay in the seventies and only slightly cooler evenings. Technically, the weather is considered a humid, subtropical climate, defined by dry warm winters and wet, humid summers.

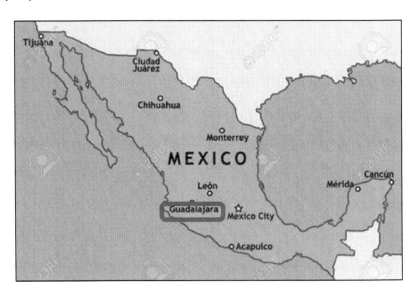

Guadalajara in Mexico [Google maps]

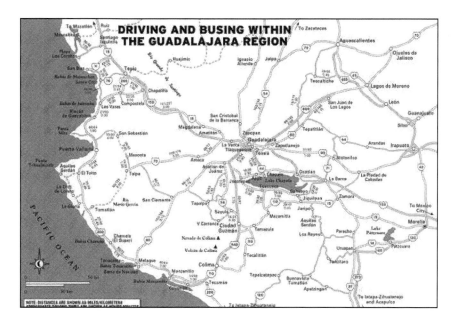

This map shows good detail of how many expat destinations relate to Guadalajara, which is also one of three major medical centers in Mexico, along with Mexico City and Monterrey.

Cancún

Cancún may be famous (or infamous) for its spring-breaks and nightlife but many expats have settled down in this easternmost city of the Yucatán peninsula, which borders on the Caribbean Sea in the Mexican state of Quintana Roo.

Having the second largest barrier reef in the world makes Cancún renowned as a top destination for scuba divers. The Pyramid of Chichen-Itza, perhaps the most famous of Mayan pyramids is located nearby, as are many other Mayan archaeological sites.

Many Mexican nationals own second homes in Cancún, creating an unusual situation where the "snowbirds" offering the best rental opportunities will be Mexican. Expats wishing to avoid the more expensive tourist zones running along the Mayan Riviera find authentic Mexico in El Centro, Cancún's historic district.

Because internet service is so crucial to us all, it's worth noting that in Cancún, local companies may require those renting to sublease the internet contract if signing a long-term lease where the internet is not automatically included.

Local online paper: *"The Playa Times" Cancún in Mexico*

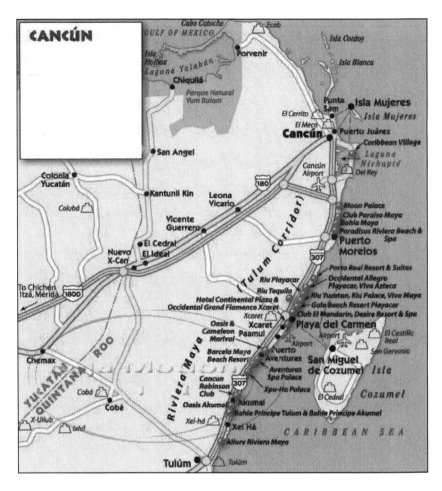

Cancún the city [Google Maps]

<u>Weather</u>: Cancún has a tropical wet and dry climate with little temperature differences between seasons, but heavy rainy seasons. Annual rainfall is around 52.8 inches. Unlike inland areas of the Yucatán Peninsula, sea breezes keep the temperatures a bit lower in the summer. More temperate conditions occur from November to February with occasional refreshing northerly breezes.

Rental concierge: Indra Rojo Chapman

Indra Rojo Chapman
Indrarojo : INDRAROJOSKYPE
Indrarojo@yahoo.com
http://www.facebook.com/LoveCancun2010/

A little about Indra: Indra is a "go to" person for Cancún and Merída, having lived for 20 years in Mexico and gone through every phrase of life there. Completely bi-lingual (she translates for a living), Indra created a Facebook page with cultural and environmental tips for people in Cancún, and it's quite popular. Feel free to check it out. http://www.facebook.com/LoveCancun2010/

What Indra loves about Cancún: I have been living in Cancún for 20 years and love everything about it. Both my children were born here. As a very active and social person, I know many people in Cancún and could be quite helpful to anyone who moves here or will be staying awhile.

Mérida - (Yucatán)

Mérida, the capital of the State of Yucatán has a fast growing and tight-knit expat community. About 30 minutes inland from Yucatán's 200-mile coastline, is well-connected by land to other parts of Mexico and to the U.S by air. The city does have an international airport and high quality medical care.

Mérida's proximity to the archaeological wonders of Chichen Itza, Uxmal, and lesser-known Mayan sites make it an excellent springboard for day trips throughout the region. The state's Mayan history casts a strong shadow upon the city's cultural offerings and general ambiance. One of Mexico's most important museums, the Gran Museo del Mundo Maya, is ultra-modern, with four large permanent exhibitions that house over 1,000 Mayan relics.

This active and safe city is notable for its textiles and cactus string hammocks. A well-organized lay-out of the grid with even numbered streets running north-south; odd numbers east-west make it unusually easy to navigate for a Mexican historical city (leave it to the Mayans).

Nearby Tulum is known for its famous aquamarine cenotes, Mayan sites, and beautiful beaches. Cancún and Tulum are both located in the bordering state of Quintana Roo but within striking distance of Mérida.

Cancún is between 4-6 hours from Mérida depending on whether you go by bus or car.

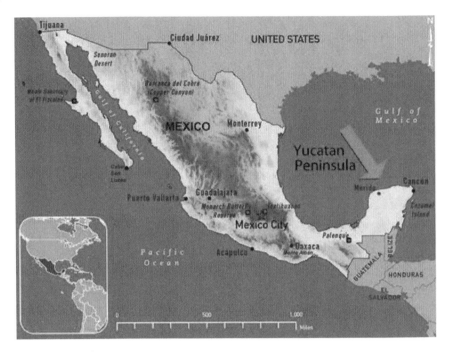

[Google maps]

Weather: Mérida's climate is hot and its humidity moderate to high, depending on the time of year. Temperatures range from 82 ° in January to 97 °F in May. Temperatures often rise to 100 °F in the summer. Low temperatures range between 64 to 73 °F in the summer. The rainy season runs from June through October.

Recommended websites: *Yucatan Living* (online and print newspaper).
A recommended rental agency: Yucatan Vacation Home Rentals & Property Management

Rental concierges
Albania Kuri Hernandez/Bárbara Vazquez and Daniella Barrera

Albania Kuri Hernandez
kuri.hdez@mextage.com

Associate: Bárbara Reyna Vazquez

E-mail: reyna.vazquez@mexstage

Mexstage (www.mexstage.com)

Yucatan

999 315 5772

Skype: Mexstage

<u>A little about Albania and Bárbara</u>: Albania and her associate Bárbara are two delightful bilingual professionals with Mexstage, which provides relocation services, immigration and legal services, "settling-in" and cultural orientation services.

Daniella Barrera

Yucatan Concierge (yucatanconcierge.com)

52 1 552 559 8547

52 999 923 3597

Skype: yucatan.concierge

E-mail: daniela@yucatanconcierge.com

<u>A little about Daniella</u>: Daniella is an ambitious and hard-working bilingual professional with excellent experience working with expats through her own concierge company, which offers traditional concierge services. She loves increasing her understanding of expats' needs. You can always be completely candid with Daniella about your questions and concerns.

See also: Indra Rojo Chapman (under "Cancún," as she goes to Merída frequently).

Guanajuato

Guanajuato is a picturesque city of color; pink and green sandstone buildings are included among those of every palette. Situated in a narrow valley, the city's tight cobble-stoned streets and alleys follow the valley's irregular terrain, making it largely impossible to drive in but creating a more European feel, with smaller yet more numerous plazas than many Mexican colonial cities. Traffic moves under the city largely by underground tunnels.

People who live here do a lot of walking and climbing of its the steep hills made a bit more challenging by the city's relatively high altitude of 6,500 feet. The city has good public transportation and cabs are plentiful. The homes and apartments are often situated off alleys, which are closed to traffic. Many of the alleys themselves have their own romantic histories.

Only a thousand or so expats live in Guanajuato proper. Others prefer to live in the flatter, more vehicle friendly communities like Marfil and La Presa outside the city. The closest international airport is in León, only 20 minutes away.

While only 50 miles from San Miguel de Allende, Guanajuato has a more youthful feel owing to the presence of thousands of students who live there most of the year and attend the University of Guanajuato. They make their presence known through roving singing parties ("callejoneadas") and abundant music.

The city hosts the Festival Internacional Cervantino, an international celebration of the arts named after Miguel de Cervantes. Cultural venues such as Juárez Theater the Teatro Principal, the Cervantes Theater, and facilities of the University provide ample plays and events.

Website (Spanish): http://www2.segundamano.mx

Where Guanajuato is in relation to the country [Google maps]

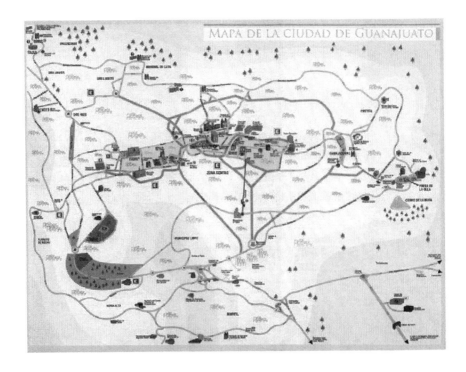

<u>Weather:</u> The area's weather is considered temperate and most homes don't have heat or air conditioning. Temperatures may get to the nineties in the summer but usually not below 60 degrees in the winter. The average temperature is 65 degrees Most rain falls between July and August and annual rainfall is about 24 to 33 inches.

Mazatlán

Do you want beautiful ocean views? Do you want city plazas with traditional Mexican charm? Do you want a vibrant arts and culture community? Mazatlán has all those things and is still remarkably affordable. Mexican nationals flock here for their own summer seaside vacations.

You can find live music practically every night and expats can choose between three lifestyles. Gated communities face golf courses or circle the Marina area at the north of the city. El Centro, at the southern end of the city, contains beautiful traditional Mexican homes and the 1920's-era Ángela Peralta Theater, a cultural hub that hosts opera, ballet, and concerts. The Theater houses renowned schools in the performing arts for aspirants from all over Latin America. Between the two areas is the Zona Dorado, on the Malecón and loaded with restaurants and bars that cater to every taste.

What locals love about Mazatlán, in the Mexican state of Sinaloa on the Pacific-side of Mexico and about six hours north of Puerta Vallarta, is that it's still a working Mexican town. Shrimp, not tourism, is the city's chief industry. Mazatlán is also known for its game fishing. The city retains a type of scruffiness reminiscent of San Diego in the 60's and is on an upswing.

Transport connections include an international airport with direct flights to key U.S. cities (and onward connections to Europe) and a highway leading north to Los Mochis and the U.S. border. The road south leads to Puerto Vallarta and then to Guadalajara, Mexico's second-largest city with excellent medical care.

Useful online papers: *Mazatlán Life, Vida Maz,* and the *Pacific Pearl*

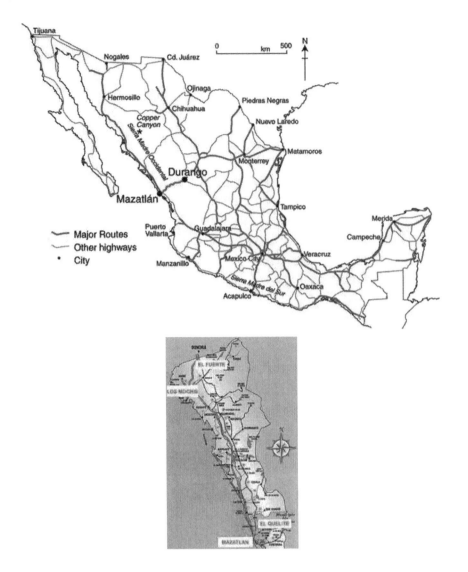

[Google maps]

Weather: The climate is dry-wet and tropical, ranging from 65 degrees in the winter to days in the mid-nineties that feel hotter because of the humidity. The year-round average is 81 degrees. Winters offer warm days and cool, somewhat humid nights. The rainy season is from July through September when sometimes-violent tropical thunderstorms are common at night. Mazatlan is subject to hurricanes from the Pacific Ocean but is protected by the Baja California peninsula.

Rental concierges: Elise Page and Veronica Erickson

Elise Page
2 Angels (4U) property management, concierge and pet services
Maz cell: #(044)6691-39-32-82
Maz Landline: #(669)176-7109 Canada Vonage Line: #(604)628-2431
Info @2angels4u.com
WWW.2ANGELS4U.COM

A little about Elise and Veronica (full disclaimer, Elise is my business partner). Elise visited Mazatlán with her parents from Canada when she was twelve and announced to them she was going to move there. At 21 she did just that and worked her way up. Almost 15 years later, she is the owner of a successful property-management company.

An absolute fanatic about Mazatlán and Mexico, Elise is bi-lingual and completely integrated into both the expat and Mexican communities. Veronica (a close friend of Elise's) also works for a real estate and property management company. She has lived in Mazatlán over 13 years and is married to a Mexican national.

Morelia

Morelia, a city of about one million people between Mexico City and Guadalajara, is difficult to categorize. A regional center, the city depends neither on expats nor tourism, although it does get plenty of both.

It is one of the most beautiful and European cities in Mexico and considered its "most Spanish" due to the restrictions on modifying building facades in its historical districts. The most salient feature distinctive to Morelia is the enormous 17th-century aqueduct running down the center of Avenida Acueducto.

Expats here keep a low profile and even their numbers are not clear. They shy away from being categorized apart from the rest of the city and remain more aloof to the community activism promoted in expat destinations like Lake Chapala and San Miguel de Allende. The city is described by residents as calm and tranquil.

Morelia's nightlife is sedate but the city still offers plenty in the way of cultural festivals and music. The Guanajuato Cervantes Festival celebrates a Morelia extension bringing in a wide variety of international events. One of the oldest music schools in the hemisphere, the Conservatory of Music offers a constant supply of recitals and productions. The Santuario de Guadalupe houses a series of 17th-century oil paintings that depict the Spanish missionaries' religious conquest of the Aztecs.

If shopping is your thing, Morelia competes well with major expat areas, a major source being Casa de Artesanias, located at an ex-convent only a few blocks from the Cathedral, which stocks the best of Michoacan crafts. The Mercado de Dulces features candy as well as inexpensive souvenirs. The Museo de Dulces hosts demonstrations in candy-making as well.

Buses, combis, and taxis form Morelia's public transport system. Whereas Mazatán has its pulmonias, Morelian has its combis, mini-vans with their destinations given on the windshields. Morelia's international airport has daily flights to the U.S and regular commuter service to Mexico City and Guadalajara.

You can use Morelia as a jumping point to Patzcuaro, Janitzio, Santa Clara del Cobre (Villa Escalante), Capula and the Monarch Butterfly Sanctuary.

Like Mazatlán, Morelia has the ill fortune to be located in a Mexican state which has received a great deal of attention for its narco-traffic and related violence. Because most people can't make the distinction between a state and a select area (i.e. the difference between living in Detroit and living in Michigan), Morelia will probably never attract huge expat numbers, although it has a great deal to recommend it. Dicey parts of the state are generally no closer than a 4-hour drive away and tended to be deep in the countryside, whereas Morelia is quiet and peaceful.

Weather: Like Puebla, Morelia offers something for the expat who prefers cooler weather, having a fall-like climate and seasons. The warmest and driest months are from May to early July. The rainy season begins in July and ends in November, characterized by brief afternoon downpours. December and January can be quite cold. Morelia nights are chilly year-round.

Rental Concierge: Tina Marie Ernspiker

Tina Marie Ernspiker
www.gringoslocos6.com
gringoslocos6@gmail.com
Facebook: https://www.facebook.com/gringoslocos6

<u>A little about Tina Marie</u>: Tina has a popular blog about Mexico through the eyes of a family of six. You can learn all about her and her crazy life on both the blog and her Facebook page.

<u>What Tina loves about Morelia and Uruapan:</u> That they are beautiful mountain cities located in the heart of Michoacan!

Oaxaca

Oaxaca City (pronounced "wa-HA-ka") is the capital of the state of the same name. Also located in a valley, Oaxaca is steeped in indigenous cultures represented by the city's 16 ethnic groups, each with its own language, dress, song, and cuisine. These groups come together to celebrate their diverse cultures at the Guelaguetza Festival, unrivaled by of festivals of its kind in Mexico.

The area is particularly known for its cuisine, which many say is the best in Mexico, typified by its mole negro, made with chocolate. In fact, chocolate in every form is sold throughout the city.

The Zocalo plaza is one of the main gathering places and the city itself is loaded with cafes, western-style saloons, galleries, small businesses, and restaurants.

One unusual cultural museum is housed in monks' cells at Santo Domingo monastery. Contemporary art is shown at Museo de Arte Contemporaneo de Oaxaca (MACO) and archaeological treasures can be found at Museo Rufino Tamayo. Archaeological sites like Monte Alban and Mitla Prehispanic Zapotec ruins are peppered throughout the region.

The city's population is very welcoming of expats, who become acquainted through activities arranged by the Oaxaca Lending Library, a very active social center. Expats are drawn to Oaxaca for its high level of safety, as it's believed to be one of the safest cities in Mexico.

The Red Cross Clinic is considered the best place to go for regular medical care. Oaxaca has an international airport. The city is about 300 miles from Mexico City and five hours from the beach.

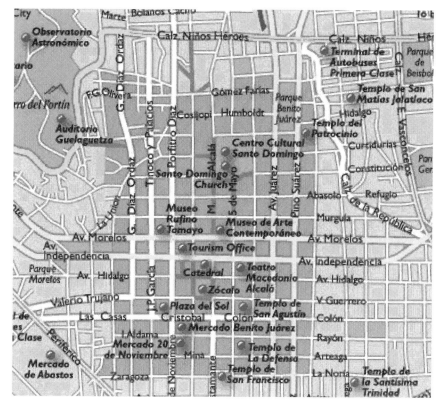

[Google maps]

Weather: The city's elevation 1500 meters above sea level gives it a mild climate year-round. The winters run between 45 and 50 degrees and the summers see 75 to 80 degrees. City precipitation runs about 30 inches of rain a year, falling from May through September, generally in the afternoons.

Rental concierge: José Santos

José Santos
Josesantosfineart@gmail.com
0052 (951) 3314927

A little about José: José Santos would be someone you'd love to know in Oaxaca. As an artist who recently returned to his home town from England, he has shown his work at three solo exhibitions and eight group exhibitions there and gave workshops in prestigious museums in same.

<u>What José loves about Oaxaca:</u> "This is a place that I treasure due to the great cultural spirit that envelops this magical southern Mexican state."

Puerto Vallarta

The iconic movie, "Night of the Iguana" with Richard Burton and Elizabeth Taylor launched Puerta Vallarta as one most popular beach resorts in Mexico decades ago. Two natural rivers that flow from the mountains to the sea and jungles surround the city. More recently, jungle scenes from "Predator" with Arnold Schwarzenegger were filmed in the nearby hills.

That being said, Puerto Vallarta (population about 300,000) isn't known for the depth of indigenous culture and colonial history like many other Mexican towns. Rather, the city retains its Mexican authenticity by having been a vibrant Mexican agricultural trading hub long before becoming a tourist destination.

Located on the western Pacific Coast, like Mazatlán, the city's predominant feature is its long stretch of Malecón (beach strand) where a lot of the action takes place. Its El Centro is divided by a Cuale River, the north part showcasing shopping, a cluster of galleries and clubs.
This part is older and full of restaurants, flea markets and offers better prices for dining and home buying. Like San Miguel de Allende, the area has steep hills to climb, which may be a consideration for some retirees.

As a popular tourist town for North Americans as well as Mexican nationals from Guadalajara and Mexico City, you have all the resort activities you could desire; from bungee-jumping, bull-fighting, deep-sea fishing, diving, shopping, fine and casual restaurants, and active nightlife.

The area is becoming known for medical tourism. Puerto Vallarta attracts a large number of expats who still find Puerta Vallarta to be an excellent deal in terms of cost of living for a coastal city, although probably more expensive than Miguel de Allende, which also ranks particularly highly among expats.

Safety (mainly petty crime) may be a bit more of an issue here, and expats are advised towards gated, secured areas. Puerto Vallarta competes with Guadalajara for the title of "San Francisco of Mexico," for being the most gay-friendly city in the country.

Helpful website: https://vallartalifestyles.com
Paradise Properties - Kelsey and Tim are recommended in several expat forums where locals share information.

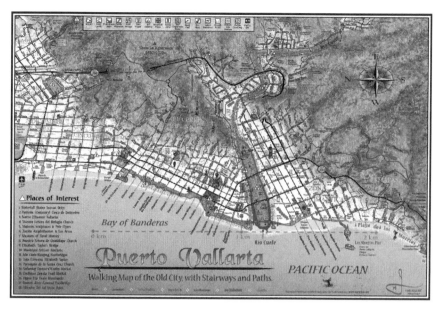

[Google maps]

Weather: Tropical wet and dry climate, The average daily high temperature is 86 degrees; average daily low temperature is 70 degrees. The rainy season extends from mid-June through mid-October, with most of the rain between July and September, especially August. Unlike Mazalán to the north, the water remains warm year round and winters are drier.

Rental concierges: Katie O'Grady

Katie O'Grady
Blog: Los O'Gradys in Mexico
E-mail: losogradysinMexico@gmail.com
http://www.losogradysinmexico.com
Serves La Cruz de Huanacaxtle, Nayarit, Bahia de Banderas Jalisco/Nayarit area including Puerto Vallarta, La Cruz, Punta Mita, Sayulita and San Pancho

A little about Katie: I call Katie, "Katie Everywhere," because of her active online presence, spreading the good word about Mexico and its lifestyle and running her relocation consulting business.

Manzanillo

Manzanillo was described to me by its rental concierge as a small fishing village on the Pacific, not a major expat destination. At a little over 100,000 people, it is a top resort destination in the state of Colima, Mexico. Predictably, it hosts major international fishing competitions and it a spot for great snorkeling and diving. It's a busy port for cruise ships as well as fishing and has two peaceful bays. Colima is about an hour away for cultural events and entertainment.

While not as pretty as Puerto Vallarta, for those seeking ocean view living (and perhaps good golfing) on a budget, Manzanillo could be a good, tranquil option.

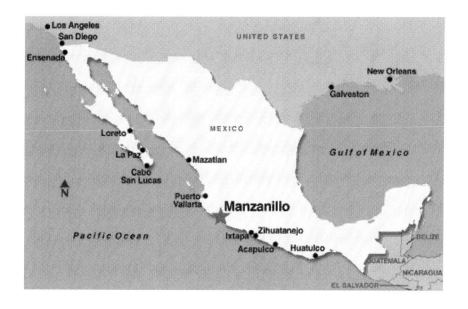

<u>Weather:</u> The dry season goes from November to May and temperatures tend to be cooler than in the wet season. The average temperature in March, the coolest month, is 75 degrees. The wet season from June to October, is warmer, averaging 83 °degrees.

Rental Concierge: Jan Golik

Jan Golik
jang1028@comcast.net
Mexico landline - (315) 351-7445
Vonage land line (free calls from USA and Canada) (408) 876-4459

San Miguel de Allende

Many an aspiring expat has expected to tour the entirety of Mexico for the "right place." When the first place they visit is San Miguel de Allende, however, they often feel they need go no further.

Clearly, there is some kind of magic to this city of a little over 140,000 people that has attracted Americans since after World War II.

The attraction that artists have to the city has been attributed to its glow and light. After World War II, veterans starting going to art schools there on the G.I. bill. The city has continued to nurture from that an ever- thriving art community. Studios and galleries, along with centers offering courses and workshops for aspiring artists keep the vibe going.

San Miguel de Allende's establishment in the art world was due largely to the efforts of a Chicago art student who is still celebrated as a hero to the city as much as the Mexican leader of Mexican Independence, Ignacio Allende, from whom the attached "de Allende" is derived.

Since then, the expats have just kept coming. San Miguel de Allende is home to over 15,000 expats, many living well in the historic area.

Being only 170 miles northwest of Mexico City in Mexico's hilly central highlands, San Miguel de Allende is also a favored destination for wealthier Mexicans who have vacation and second homes there.

Many high-end restaurants and hotels cater to the well-heeled tourist. The city has excellent clinics and for more serious conditions, people can also travel to nearby Querétaro. The nearest international airports are in León and Mexico City.

San Miguel de Allende's weather makes the city perfect for a proliferation of rooftop bars and restaurants with excellent views of the city. Narrow cobblestone streets, lush courtyards, baroque architecture and stunning sunsets framed by the nearby Sierra Madre Mountains make many consider San Miguel de Allende as the most beautiful town in Mexico.

The many events (such as Fashion Days in March and November attracts Mexico's top designers and a major international film festival), festivals, parades (Las Calle-joneadas being the most popular) and fireworks that go on in the city year-round are measured in relation to their distance from El Jardín, the principal plaza, and the Parroquia, the large church, at its heart.

San Miguel de Allende hosts Mexico's second-largest English library and the bilingual *Atención San Miguel* which is published in the library is a must-read for what's going on in the city.

All this magic has made San Miguel de Allende pricier than other expat destination cities. Younger and new expats are still finding affordable homes and apartments outside the city's center, in communities like Independencia, San Antonio, and Guadalupe.

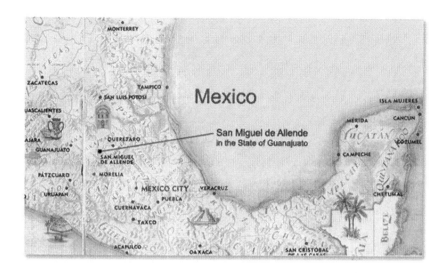

San Miguel de Allende's position in Mexico [Google maps]

San Miguel de Allende

<u>Weather:</u> San Miguel de Allende has spring-like weather near year-round with lowest temperatures hovering around 34F at night in the winter and 75F in the summer during the day. The year-round average is 66 degrees. The rainy season runs from late May to October each year, with some heavy tropical storms.

Rental Concierge

Adriana Torres Solis
Telephone: 044 415 103 9962
Email: adriana.toso9@gmail.com
Skype: aristoso9 / Aris Torres

A little about Aris: Aris was born in San Miguel de Allende and knows "every corner" of the city. For eight years she has worked as an agent with a local real estate company. She is bi-lingual.

<u>What Aris loves about San Miguel de Allende:</u> "I assure you that there is nothing like falling in love and living in San Miguel. Walking downtown in the early hours of the morning will make you feel like you have it all."

Puebla

Southwest of Mexico City and about two hours from Cuernavaca in the state of Morelos, Puebla is located in the Valley of Cue Tlaxcoapan, a large valley surrounded on four sides by the mountains and the Trans-Mexican volcanic belt, which give residents a spectacular view of the snow-covered peaks, particularly the Popocatepetl and Iztaccihuatl volcanoes. The nearby mountains offer opportunities for scenic picnics, hiking, mountain-biking, and more extreme sports like paragliding.

Mexico's fourth-largest city of 1.5 million is largely undiscovered by expats which mean rentals and home prices are still quite low, even around the most popular areas such as the main plaza and center of cultural life, El Zocalo. In spite of its size and being host to a number of prestigious universities, Puebla retains a smaller town feel, with restaurants often closing early on weeknights.

Puebla has a healthy middle class and many wealthy Mexican residents so goods and services are available in all ranges of prices. Exquisite ceramics, called Talavera, are made here, a style introduced from Spain centuries ago upon the discovery of the region's fine clay. Callejón de los Calle Callejón de los Sapos, (Frog Alley) offers an abundance of antique dealers, artisanal vendors and furniture sellers.

Puebla's concentration of Baroque, Renaissance and Classic architecture has bequeathed it the "Cradle of Mexican Baroque." Even if you think you've seen enough of the abundance of cathedrals in Mexico, Puebla Catedral de Puebla is widely considered the finest in Mexico, constructed in 1575 and inspired by St. Peter's Basilica.

You can't really talk about Puebla without mentioning the food, particularly the *Molé Poblano* and *chile en nogada*, which were invented here. Other classics are *ch-*

alupas (fried corn tortilla topped with salsa, onions, and shredded meat), *tingas* (a chipotle-laced chicken stew), and *tacos árabe* (shawarma-style pork on flatbread). Puebla loves its sweets too. An entire street, the so-called Calle de los Dulces (Sweet Street) also known as La Calle de Santa Clara, sells the region's candies such as *camote, muégano,* and *las tortitas de Santa Clara.*

Puebla offers art galleries as well as museums with colonial and modern art. Particularly notable is the Museo Amparo where a duo of colonial buildings houses one of the finest collections of Mexican art in Latin America.

The Teatro Principal de Puebla hosts cultural events and art shows featuring regional, national and international artists. Perhaps the point of interest most unusual for a Mexican city is the *teleférico,* or cable car, which offers a suspended journey above the city so you can take in the views of the colonial town.

World-class hospitals are available in Puebla complemented by an extensive network of privately owned hospitals and outpatient clinics. English-speaking physicians are readily on hand in Puebla although the city does not have a large American or Canadian expat population. Puebla is near Cuernavaca, a popular expat and tourist destination.

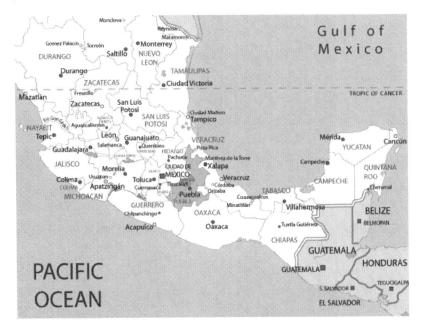

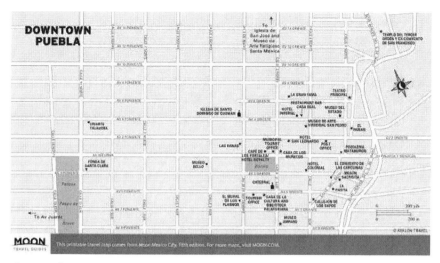

[Google maps]

<u>Weather:</u> Any expat who seeks a cool, dry and mosquito-free retirement should take a look at the City of Puebla. The climate is moderated by its high altitude (7,217.85 ft) so Puebla rarely gets truly hot. Night temperatures are always cool at all times of the year, usually cool enough for extra clothing. The dry season runs from November through April. Rainy season from May–October.

Rental concierge: Cesár Dorantes Benitez

Cesár Dorantes Benitez
residenciasuniversitariaslapaz@hotmail.com
E-mail: cdorant@itesm.mx
Skype: live:dorantescesar
Phone numbers: 045 222 505 1091
From Mexico: 222 505 1091

<u>A little about Cesár:</u> Cesár is a family man with a wife and daughter and works in student affairs at the Tecnologico de Monterrey, one one of most prestigious universities in Mexico. He spent 11 years in New York and Washington D.C. as an adult.

<u>What Cesár loves about Puebla (and a little-known fact)</u>: "Many universities and professional institutes have opened careers in food related areas so in the last few years we have had many students who have graduated in gastronomic careers. Many of them have started to work in local restaurants so it's common to eat in a non-pre-suming restaurant and find out that the food is excellent!"

Cuernavaca/Morelos

Often overlooked, Cuernavaca has more to offer tourists and retirees at lower cost than most anywhere else in Mexico. The resort city lies just 90 minutes south of the capital and because of its near-perfect climate, this "city of eternal spring" has attracted vacationers since the days of the Aztec emperors.

Cuernavaca has always been much more popular among Mexicans than outsiders, and the local population of about 800,000 swells by the thousands on weekends and holidays. The city does have a growing cluster population of expats.

For things to do, the salons at the Borda Garden host concerts, plays and art exhibits. The Teatro Ocampo, in a beautifully renovated old movie house, has at several events a week, which may include the Morelos State Ballet, a chamber music orchestra, and visiting groups like the National Symphony.

From Cuernavaca, it's a short bus ride to the "Pueblo Mágico" de Tepoztlán, the ancient Hacienda Cocoyoc, the ruins of Xochicalco, or the silver city of Taxco. San Miguel de Allende is about four hours away.

One of the biggest advantages of this city is the availability of good medical and dental facilities. including well-trained, English-speaking specialists in cardiology, gastroenterology, obstetrics, plastic surgery, and optometry (including laser surgery). Its National School of Public Health is one of the most prestigious in the Americas.

Inside the city are green retreats such as the San Anton waterfall, La Borda city gardens, and Chapultepec ecological park that features springs, picnic areas, and a small zoo. Five miles outside the city are hiking trails, horseback riding, crystal-clear springs and lagoons for swimming, boating, and freshwater fishing, and camping. Some of the local spas are rated as being the finest in Mexico.

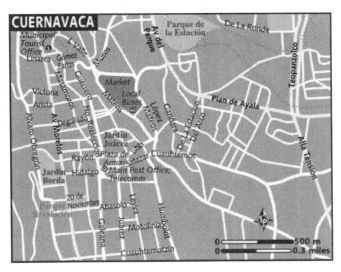

[Google maps]

<u>Weather:</u> The climate here is one of the best in the world, with a mean temperature of 75 degrees and more than 300 days of sunshine. Spring arrives in early February with daytime temperatures in the 80s falling to 65 at night until May, the hottest month, when the temperature does occasionally soar. In June through mid-October, cooling rains arrive.

Rental Concierges: Christopher/Patricia Hoffman and Ana Paula Aguirre Hall

Christopher Kerr Hoffman
And mother, **Patty Hoffman**
Home phone +52(777)313_7331
Patty's WhatsApp +52(777)787_9256
Christopher's WhatsApp +52(777)161-0373
Christopher's email: christopherkerr87@hotmail.com
E-mail: pattyaqui@yahoo.com.**mx**
Skype: pattyaqui
Serves Cuernavaca

<u>A little about Patty:</u> Patty and her son, Christopher will make a great team for you. He was born in Mexico and their family represents the gentle spirit of Mexico.

<u>What she loves about Cuernavaca:</u> I love Cuernavaca because of its beautiful climate and beautiful flowers all year-long and, most important, I love it of all for the wonderfully nice people who live here.

Ana Paula Aguirre Hall
Cuernavaca
Email: aguirrehall@yahoo.com.**mx**
Cell: 777- 206 6655
Skype: ana.paula.aquirre

<u>A little about Ana:</u> Ana is a former property manager, bilingual (Mexican national) and understands expat expectations and the Mexican culture, giving her a perfect blend of experience.

<u>What she loves about Cuernavaca</u>: "I love living in Cuernavaca mostly because of its wonderful weather, the lush vegetation, and its closeness to Mexico City. It has amazing historic buildings and is surrounded by pyramids and great archeological sites. It is also located at a 3-hour distance from the fantastic beach city of Acapulco."

Mexico City

I'm sure that Mexico City has many expats too. As a more expensive and complicated beast (24 million souls living there), we're going to focus on the common destinations in the city descriptions. (When even Mexican nationals who were born there call it, "The Jungle," the chances are good Mexico City is quite different from Lake Chapala or Mérida).

For tips on how to rent out your home or apartment in the U.S., read my blog on the subject on the Ventanas Mexico website: www.ventanasmexico.com, "Expat Life and Your Housing Plan: The Secrets of Subletting Your Place."

Chapter One

The Master Plan - Living in Mexico for less

How would you like to live in an upscale house or beachfront condo in Mexico for six to eight months a year for less than you pay for a vanilla apartment anywhere in the U.S?

You could do this every year for as many years as it takes to decide whether to relocate permanently. You could live part of the year in Mexico while still keeping a U.S. or Canadian footprint and reduce your yearly living expenses to boot (pardon the pun).

To build a life lived between two countries for considerably less than you'd spend living in one requires finding great places to live year after year, a system.

Over the years, my business partner (who has 10 years as a property manager in Mexico) and I have learned a good bit about renting in Mexico.

This book will focus on medium term rentals, periods of three months to up to a year, less time than would typically require a lease. However, much of the information applies to longer leases too, which we also touch on.

While 100% the numbers in this book may not apply 100% of the time, most will hold true no matter where you go, regardless of when an area's low and high season is. Much of this advice you won't find on the web and you most certainly won't hear it from realtors and those who make a living renting to North Americans.

Chapter Two

Renting in Mexico is different from renting in the U.S. or Canada

Many factors affecting your choice of places won't be mentioned by realtors because they are culturally-based and can be delicate topics to wade into.

After having lived and rented in Mexico for a number of years and season, it surprises me how many websites that otherwise give accurate information on Mexico make the rental process sound as straightforward as it is in the U.S.

While it may look that way on the surface when working with realtors, a lot of latitude exists that can save you considerable money.

One difficulty in researching Mexico is that so many processes here are fungible. You may read up on say, how to set up a bank account in Mexico, walk into a bank, and find that you are asked for a completely different set of documents. Arrangements often depend on the perspective of the players. Renting is the same.

A whole underground rental market exists beyond what you'll find on rental websites. Spectacular places on Rent by Owner and realtor sites receive top dollar, only practical for a vacation or if you have a big budget. A whole separate market exists for those who know it is there, beautiful places rented out only by referral and word of mouth.

These home and condo owners do not advertise that they rent their places out because of tax implications, homeowner association rules, or out of fear of drawing the wrong tenant. I'd estimate as many as 50% of expat rentals are made by word of mouth, social media, and arrangements between "friends," carefully vetted.

Chapter Three

Deciding where to live in Mexico

The web is full of lists of the top places to live in Mexico. Most people prefer at least some expat presence in the cities they are considering. If you don't speak fluent Spanish, living in other than the top 15 or so of the most popular areas for expats would most likely be a mistake (I never say "never").

You should always rent for a few years before buying a place, an opinion I hold from my own experiences as well as one almost unanimously expressed online by expats. You can't really understand the nuances in property values without living in a city a few years. Houses may seem inexpensive but are high for the market.

Without time in an area, it's easy to over-invest in your "dream" Mexican home and not be able to sell it quickly or re-coup your money should you unexpectedly have to return to the U.S. or you want to try a different Mexican city. Buying in Mexico is easy. Selling not so much.

Chapter Four

Go In Big: The advantages of a position of strength in selecting the first place you live

Once you have picked your top prospective city, you will want to plan at least a one to three- month stay before making the longer commitment. A year in the wrong place can be a *very* long time.

Yes, you can find nice apartments and homes from $400 -$700 a month in all the cities listed in this book. My advice is to invest a little more if necessary in the front end (your initial stay) for safety and social reasons. One of the wisest things I did in my first few years was rent the most spacious, attractive and welcoming flats I could afford to rent (all in the $850-$950 range, all oceanfront).

Think about executives who move to new towns. They need to make contacts. They obtain places where they can entertain. You need to do the same thing - even more so.

In the first few years, you have to make the contacts necessary to a foundation for a happy life in Mexico. Whether you are full or part-time, making Mexican friends of good character (whether you speak Spanish or they speak English) will make your life in Mexico easier, cheaper, safer, and tons more fun.

Mexicans like to visit people's homes. They like to hang out in places other than bars and restaurants. So do I. Probably so do you. Having an especially attractive place where you can host modest dinners, or even offer to host a book club meeting for them will go a long way towards making native local friends.

Having a house or flat with a little something special to attract guests is one of the easiest ways to reciprocate for all the advice and help Mexicans and resident expats are likely to provide you over the course of your acclimating to a new country. Treat them well.

If your Spanish skills are nascent and you want to improve those language skills, invite a couple of Mexicans over at the same time. Cooking dinner or making tapas while they talk will take the conversational pressure off you. Mexicans are the warmest, most generous people in the world.

If you don't plan on learning the language at all, new expat acquaintances like to see other people's places and get a sense of who you are too. Mexicans who speak English like to practice their language skills in social occasions. Having an attractive, spacious place facilitates opportunities to make the many types of friends you'll need to get the most out of expat life.

Just like an extra $200 rent a month can make a considerable difference in the quality of an apartment in the U.S., even $100 a month more can take you up a few notches in Mexico.

Once your social infrastructure, language skills and your comfort level of living in Mexico develops fully, you can always cut back on rent. You will know by then when and how to reduce costs without reducing your standard of living. You will have developed a comfort level with different neighborhoods. Most importantly, you will have a nucleus of friends, a network. If you follow the advice in this book, you will be able to uncover luxurious places that are also very affordable, year after year.

Chapter Five: Online rental listings

Take caution in choosing rental listing sources

Be cautious when considering sites such as Craigslist or Ebay. One of the worst experiences my business partner, a property manager, ever had was helping a Mexican family who booked a stay at a condominium complex through Ebay, the online consumer-to-consumer sales business.

The condo complex existed. In fact, I lived in it myself. The specific apartment did not. This poor family spent more than thousand dollars and saw their beautiful vacation property only to find out their booking was made in thin air.

A criminal can throw up a fake property rental website complete with sophisticated booking features in a week-end these days. Taking precautions on these sites is no different from the same you should take in the U.S., which has its own full share of similar scams.

Below are a few excellent sources of rentals. You will need a friend or a concierge to check the place out before making any financial commitment.

In Spanish
http://www.locanto.com.mx
http://www.vivanuncios.com.mx/
http://www.olx.com.mx/
http://mexico.inmobiliaria.com/
https://www.sublet.com/

In English

Tripping.com
Booking.com
Homeaway.com

Chapter Six: Using a realtor

Choose carefully

The frightening prospect of bogus rental sites may convince you to use a traditional realtor to find a place for your first stay. Using realtors is sometimes the best thing to do. I have used a realtor to rent a place before. She and her husband were terrific.

As you consider your choice of realtors, consider this too. Unlike in the U.S., service businesses have few regulatory restrictions in Mexico. Professional associations have no teeth to enforce ethics violations. Honest business practices are more *voluntary*, you might say. Most realtors are professional and honest, but be aware that it's easier for them to do business in Mexico than the U.S. even if they are not.

You also will be vulnerable to the "halo effect." The halo effect is a common cognitive bias, a type of confirmation bias where positive feelings about a trait (speaking English, or being from your country in this case) causes other traits to be viewed more positively than they would otherwise.

How the bias manifests in Mexico is that newcomers are so relieved to find a fellow countryman, that American and Canadian service providers appear more competent.

The halo effect not only affects how people choose realtors. You will see it and perhaps even experience it yourself when deciding among many service vendors, from hairdressers to computer repair people.

Aware of the bias, some American and Canadian service providers in Mexico take advantage of it by charging more than Mexican providers (Mexican providers can speak English too, you know) for the same services. My Mexican hairdresser shakes her head in wonder at the high prices her Canadian competitor charges her fellow Canadians.

Character and honesty are obviously an individual traits. There are just as many horror stories about Canadian and American realtors as Mexican ones. For example, a couple who are friends of mine in Mexico signed a year rental contract right after arriving in Mexico with an American realtor only to find their house would never have hot water. Their countryman never looked back.

Before you commit, talk to people who have used that realtor. Check online forums for recommendations and complaints. With legal recourse unlikely, you have to rely much more on reputation and referrals from locals familiar with the market. Reputation weighs in much heavier when doing business in Mexico. This applies across the board in all service industries and once again proves why time and contacts in a city are so important.

Aren't realtors' commissions paid by the homeowner?

One high-traffic site on Mexico recommends in its section about renting to use realtors because "The owner pays the realtor's commission."

That may be true but the statement is misleading. The owner makes up for that commission by building it into your rent. At its fairest, commissions both increase the amount you pay and decrease the property owners profit.

They can be the best course of action and worth the fee. But if you are coming to Mexico for several years, even the ones whom you like and trust won't always have the type of place you want in their inventory at the very best price.

Start calling around during low season months to take the frenzy out of the negotiation process. Realtors are good at playing up a "better take it now because the city is filling up!" sense of urgency in the weeks leading up to the high season.

Don't be conned. Beautiful empty places are all over the place in towns with low seasons. You should be able to pick and choose if you understand how electricity is billed, and don't mind a little heat or rain, and know how to promote yourself as a great tenant.

VRBO charges between 5-12% for their service fee. Although they say the "traveler" pays the fee, again, not really because it affects the rent they can ask and still make a reasonable profit.

Chapter Seven: Consider Mexican National Holidays

Don't forget Mexican vacation schedules when planning your stays

One of the things that I always had a problem remembering during my first few years renting in Mexico was that North Americans aren't the only tourist game in town.

Mexican coastal cities and the more beautiful cities inland have two different tourist seasons, like layers of people. The terms "on" and "off-season" generally refers to the time of year snowbirds hit town. They may stay for a month or may stay the whole season. They go home when the heat of summer or rainy season hits.

Mexicans have their own tourist seasons. Their tourist seasons are the times of year when they go on annual vacations. Just like in the U.S. they take their families to the beach during the summer, have three-day week-ends, national holidays, and Semana Santa religious weeks.

Every popular Mexican town has its own times when hordes of Mexican national tourists hit as well as the foreigners who want to experience the town's local festivals. These two layers may overlap but they do not coincide.

I know the concept of Mexicans taking their own vacations sounds like common sense as you read this, but it's really easy to forget as an expat when your own country's holidays and three-day week-ends are on different cycles.

Find out the big Mexican tourist weeks of the town you're going to. Will there be a famous local holiday during the time you are considering a long-term visit? Cities near Mexico City and Guadalajara especially get waves of Mexican national tourists on their own schedules. Cuernavaca and Puebla are also very popular for people living in Mexico City.

The more you can avoid running into prime rental seasons and weeks, the better deal you will get on your long-term rental. Once you have been in Mexico awhile, you will have plenty of time to figure out how to experience the big celebrations if you want to.

Chapter Eight: Reconnoitering

The one-month stay (for newbies)

When you go about planning your first trip, internet research will uncover a host of property rental companies and rent by owner sites like VRBO and Airbnb. Regardless of whether the listing is on VRBO, AirBnB, or listed online through a realtor, places you find online tend to be more expensive.

You are at their mercy. The price will sound great, even though probably inflated by local standards. Without intimate inside information about the locale, you won't be able to negotiate effectively because you will be thinking in term of U.S. dollars. You won't know the ebb and flow of rentals for the area at that time of year by North Americans and Mexican nationals.

In all fairness, for a one-month rental, the owners' profit margin needs to be higher, especially if they only rent it during the high season.

Reconcile yourself to the higher price of a one-month stay as a cost of doing business. Then use every day during this stay to do the research necessary to position yourself for planning the longer stay, the real test-drive of living in Mexico either as a retiree or part-time expat.

Go for that month with the sole intention of working your tail off making contacts and taking detailed notes on the names of the neighborhoods you like, the names of the buildings that appeal to you, and getting contact information on the people managing them.

Better yet, try to get the owners names (although harder information to obtain).

This info won't only pay off in your first year but will pay off *for years to come.* Don't rent a hotel room for a week. That's just not enough time.

Look at buildings, take pictures and videos from your phone and label them carefully. Take notes and place pins on maps. You may think you'll remember a place but it doesn't take long to confuse your Pueblos Bonitos with your Pueblos de las Rosas. Take your phone and call on the spot if there's a sign ("Se Renta") on a gate or in a window with a phone number on it.

This step is no vacation. You will be hot and bothered. You will look terrible. You will be exhausted by the language barrier. You will be pounding pavement day and night (the time you really want to check a neighborhood) gathering the information you'll need to be able to separate fact from fiction when you get back home and begin your real research online. Your diet will suck. This will be the worst, most uncomfortable step in creating your personal paradise in Mexico.

With hard work in your first month stay you should have made several principal contacts with permanent residents, whom you will woo shamelessly (yet sincerely, naturally) every chance you get.

You should return home with a full list of the neighborhoods you'd consider and the names of the complexes you like, with pictures, notes, and maps of where they are in the city. You just completed the hardest part of your journey. This information will reap benefits for years to come.

Consider planning your one-month visit off-season

Off season can be a great time for a one-month stay. Flights are cheaper. Rentals are less. Even a one-month rental should be cheaper than a one-month stay during high season or the most popular months.

In every expat town, you will find coffee shops, internet cafes, libraries or bars where full-time expats hang out. Get out and chat them up. These known expat hang-outs often have bulletin boards with rental postings. As you get information, maintain info in your notebook for future years.

Local permanent residents are more visible off-season. They are easier to run into and most likely live there full-time if you are seeing them in low season. Expats are easy to spot year-round but in the most popular months, they will have varying degrees of knowledge because some are snowbirds.

By going in low season, you won't be distracted by the whirling social scene and invitations made by snowbirds. You may think they'd be able to provide you all the information you need. They can't. They only know their slice of the expat experience, the most expensive slice.

I made my first one-month visit to Mexico in August. If I met someone in the grocery store or coffee shop, I could assume they were permanent residents with more thorough knowledge of the area. After one month off-season, I knew more about prices and renting in the town my snowbird friends who had been visiting for years.

Realtors and property managers are less busy. By going off season for the initial one-month reconnoitering, it will be easier to get appointments to see places you'd consider renting for your six-month stay as they will likely be unoccupied.

Going off-season, you will be somewhat of an oddity, which will play in your favor. People will remember you not as just another snowbird, but as someone a little crazier and a lot sweatier.

Chapter Nine

Go home, not crazy

After the first month there, go home and digest. You've done it. Without that month of real experience under your belt, you would not be able to separate the wheat from the chaff in your online research. Now start your research and social media campaign for your minimum five- month stay.

Researching Mexico online is more than frustrating. It is delivered via fire hose with no prioritization according to what you need to know for each particular stage of the transition. You will spend 30 minutes on a website or blog only often to see it hasn't been updated since 2009 (Thanks, Google!)

Some research, including books, will lead you to toss and turn over how to get your possessions over the border before you even know how to buy milk.

Don't over-do it.

As easy as it will be to get distracted by the article on how to re-cycle in Mexico, concentrate only the information relative to the next step: setting up a long-term, enjoyable stay in a safe area to see how you like living in Mexico, with Mexicans (They are part of the package).

Determine what you need to know to live there for six months and research answers to only those questions, not what you need to know to live there the rest of your life. Skip the story about narco-traffic dealing in Ciudad Juarez unless you're moving to Ciudad Juarez.

I made the big mistake of spending a lot of time online researching about how to live in Mexico before even making my first one month trip. All I did was scare the hell out of myself, filling myself up with anxiety about dengue fever and touching the currency.

What harm can too much research do? In addition to provoking unnecessary anxiety, when you get embedded in the minutia you tend to weigh all the information equally. Some information you need and frankly some you don't and perhaps never will.

Many things that you will have to do *someday* in Mexico sound much harder when you read about them online or in a book than when you have lived there awhile if ultimately you even do. Prioritize.

Here's a test to see if you know how to curate research properly. Which article do you read and which do you skip?

- Foreign Income Exclusion in Mexico
- How much are 1,683 pesos in U.S. dollars?

See what I mean?

You have a singular goal at this point: to secure a beautiful, safe place to live for six months to a year at an excellent price. Concentrate only on finding information pertaining to that. Otherwise, you will either go insane or spend an inordinate amount of time dreaming/researching rather than taking the first concrete step - actually living there.

Chapter Ten

Your six-month stay - plan it to incorporate off-season months as well

Your first-month reconnoitering stay should have provided you the basics on the ideal areas to live, referrals to reputable realtors, and a few good permanent resident contacts. You will need to develop a number of sources if you want to to get the best places at the best prices year after year.

Even though many expat cities have nice weather year-round, they all to some degree have months that empty out of Mexican vacationers and expats with second homes. They *all* have popular months and less popular months.

When you schedule your six month stay in Mexico, do not stay for all the months of the high season when the weather is best. If you do that, you will pay the maximum rental rates and be surrounded by snowbirds who only have part of the story.

Everyone should know what their potential Mexican home is like during its worst months. Work several shoulder months into your stay. To get the best deals on rent, you will need to include at least a few months of off-season rental.

The downside (probably the heat, or the rain) will be obvious. The upside of off-season is

1. Mexican locals who speak English well often have jobs related to tourism. They are less busy during less popular months and more available to talk.

2. As mentioned, it's more obvious who lives year-round in low season. Permanent resident expats are less busy than in more popular months when social calendars fill up as they reconnect with snowbird friends.

3. It's easier to get appointments with services. Waits at immigration offices for inquiries into Visas and other *tramites* (bureaucratic functions) are short or non-existent off-season.

4. You will have far fewer social distractions to prevent you from developing your comprehensive long-term plan for your life in Mexico, whether it's volunteering, doing remote work, setting up a business or writing the Great American Novel.

By spending at least part of the long-term stay off-season, or during a less popular time, you will have the opportunity to lock yourself up in a luxurious place, perhaps with an ocean view, and begin to visualize what you want this second life to look like.

When the weather is beautiful, it's hard not to want to play all day and it's easy to find people who will do it with you. The off-season months are when you can get things accomplished.

5. With more time indoors you can, and should, study some Spanish. You can't learn the language by osmosis. The more Spanish you have, the more control you will have over your life in Mexico, not to mention all the benefits too numerous to mention here. You get more out learning Spanish in an "immersion" experience if you are complementing it with old fashioned study.

6. Summer nights in Mexican coastal towns can be magical. You can swim. You can stay up all night and watch violent tropical thunderstorms come in over the ocean. In coastal areas, you see things snowbirds never see.

Perhaps the most important reason to stay at least several months off season is the leverage you have when negotiating rental rates.

7. By going partly off-season, you can pick and choose among the nicest places to live.

Many homeowners like the idea of generating income in low season, even if they earn a little less for the high season months that are included as well. You just have to find those homeowners.

I usually arrive in Mexico sometime between June and August and stay at least six months at a time. Arriving in these months gives me approximately four shoulder/off-season months and 1-2 high season months, enabling me to negotiate a much better rental rate.

You could also plan a stay at the tail end of the high season for a coastal area and get the same benefits. You enjoy a month or two of great weather and get a whole lot done inside during the off-season months. Resident expats sew, do online work, or catch up on reading during the hot or rainy months. They all have projects set aside for those times.

If you are not a beach person, investigate whether there are high and low seasons in the area that interests you. Low season in inland areas are the rainy months. While they may be perfectly pleasant months for the locals, those months will at least drive out the Mexican nationals and the snowbird-iest of snowbirds, clearing a little more space for you and your budget.

For example, Lake Chapala's high season (most popular months) runs from the end of September to the first part of April. The low season is defined by rainy months, months that some permanent residents have told me they love but people with second homes there may avoid.

Northern Mexico, especially around Chihuahua, or even Puebla, can be cold. They might offer similar opportunities for reduced rent in exchange for part of the stay being in their own low season. Many expats live in Mexico's highlands. Those areas don't have large expat populations, making your status as a North American tenant even that much more of a playing card (We'll get into that later).

By all means, if you love a place, know your next year's schedule and want to rent it again, reserve it again before you leave. While it's easy to find a place off-season, the high season months book quickly and in advance. You can always find good places off-season.

To get the best rate for six-months or more, you need to book low and high season months together. The goal of renting during low season and high season, along with being cheaper, is that it puts you in a better position to negotiate a much better rate for a month or two of the best months.

Book as far in advance as possible so that the high months are still available for your timeframe.

Ways to get back the cost of your flight

Dental and other services
Do you need dental work done? Dental work, routine check-ups, spa services like botox, eye appointments and contact prescriptions are all much cheaper in Mexico. Dental services in particular are one-third to half of what dentists charge in the United States. One key reason for this is that dentists in the United States often are paying off large student loans and the costs of labor and technology are so much higher.

Ask your rental concierge or expats you meet for referrals to doctors for these services if you need them. A six-month stay is plenty of time to arrange for services like this. The money you save will probably be more than the cost of your flight.

The cost of dental work in the U.S. has skyrocketed. Many expat already travel over the border for more expensive procedures, which could cost as little as a third of what is charged in the U.S. I get botox treatment, dental work, and my contact exams and prescriptions in Mexico.

VISA Tips

People initially come to Mexico on a tourist visa, which allows you 180 days in Mexico. One of the things I wished I'd done before my very first longer-term stay is go to the nearest consulate and apply for a Visa Termporal, which allows you to stay several years.

You don't apply for this visa in Mexico. You have to apply at a Mexican consulate in your home country and show assets of around $93,000 or a source of income between $1,500 - $2,200, depending on whether you are single or married. After four years, you automatically qualify for permanent resident status. At that time you also have to decide on whether you want resident status.

Once you apply at the consulate, you have a limited period before you need to check in at the closest immigration office in Mexico to finish the process, which initially takes two visits, the second one for fingerprinting.

Although the visa temporal is good for 2-4 years, you must renew it in Mexico every year. Make sure to check the date on the card so you will know how soon you have to return to Mexico to renew it. Otherwise you have to start the process all over again.

Why not apply at your consulate before your very first trip and get the ball rolling? The cost of applying is only $35. That way, in future trips, you won't be locked in to a maximum six-month time frame. If an especially good eight-month rental deal comes up in future years, your paperwork will be in order to take advantage of it.

Of course there are reasons you may want to wait, but if you are seriously considering permanent relocation and believe four years is enough time to decide, it will give you more freedom in your schedule. With a Visa Temporal, you can also apply for IMSS national healthcare insurance in Mexico, a good idea if you're living there for any length of time.

Why not be a snowbird?

Snowbirds arrive to Mexico's expat cities en masse at the height of the best weather. They pay a premium on everything even though the prices may seem low by American standards. They usually stay one to three months in what is really an extended vacation. Being more cocooned, they don't really live the expat life.

Not that snowbird life isn't great in Mexico. Snowbirds I know seem delirious with contentment. Their social agendas are full and the weather in high season can be straight-up southern-Californian, but they are not the same as you. You are considering retiring full-time to Mexico someday or making Mexico your home for at least six months a year at an affordable cost.

You can cut your yearly budget in half if you rent or sublease your permanent residence at home for the months you live in Mexico. If you aren't willing or can't do that, paying rent for three months in Mexico during the high season plus paying your own mortgage or rent makes being a snowbird an expensive proposition.

Chapter Eleven

Cultural factors that affect your rental opportunities - Owners and Renters

Now we get into the secrets of the Mexican rental market. Many expats who have rented in Mexico for years have no idea of their leverage. They arrange their lives the way they do in the U.S. They find a place they like, they ask what the rent is and because it seems like a good deal compared to home, they rent it. Most never know the difference because they are getting all their information from other expats or realtors.

You can do better. Sometimes much better. To understand why, you need to know the different types of renters and owners.

Two types of owners

You have two types of property owners in Mexico; Canadian/American owners and Mexican owners.

1. Mexican rental property owners

Mexican property owners are different from American/Canadian property owners. Most likely their rental property is an investment property or for rental income. Some Mexicans who work in the U.S. buys their future retirement homes outright years before retirement. Their relatives live close enough to keep and eye on it.

A couple of cities, notably Cancun, have a large contingent of wealthier Mexicans who own second homes there. Many would love to rent these places out short-term to a North American.

Mexican owners will hire a realtor or property manager to promote their second homes for rent if they are trying to secure a North American renter. Others stick a sign in the window or gate with "se renta." Without fluent Spanish, your risk factor renting from individuals with rental homes and units rather than using a realtor goes up. Misunderstandings are common.

With the exception of the most high-end complexes and second homes, Mexican realtors/owners often don't have a good grasp of North American expectations (The exception is couples where one spouse is Mexican and the other North American).

On the other hand, you will almost always pay less renting from a Mexican than from an expat or North American. Once you know your way around and have a few Mexican friends, you will probably want to start directing yourself towards Mexican owners if saving money is your primary concern. In order to save the the most money you will most likely need to:

- rent from a Mexican (if you don't speak Spanish, I urge you to learn if saving money in a primary motivation for considering Mexico as speaking Spanish enables you to negotiate more effectively for many services and goods).
- live without a few features common to North American apartments or homes.
- make a few inexpensive modifications on your own dime.

2. North American property owners who rent

North American property owners on the other hand, almost always have purchased the property as a second home.

Sometimes they bought the condo/apartment years ago and no longer visit as often. Sometimes the house/condo is limbo; for sale if a prospect appears. When a house is for sale, the furnishings are almost always sold with the house, making it perfect for renting if the right tenant appears and the market isn't too hot.

Properties tend to take longer to sell in Mexico. Often owners have invested too much in the home and in trying to recoup their investment, have overpriced the property for sale (and everyone in town knows it). In this situation, owners get caught with the need to rent the house out when they hadn't originally intended to.

Other North American homeowners have beautiful places and to them, it seems silly (and risky) to leave it empty and unattended for months at a time when the house could, with the right person, generate income.

These properties are often not advertised. They can be your best opportunities for rent negotiation. Owners of second homes are often open to having a longer-term North American tenant they can trust both for the income and presence on the property, particularly if the property is a stand alone home. While some with second homes use online listing services like RBO (Rent by Owner), many only rent through word of mouth for long-term stays.

Renting during the hottest months in coastal or hotter regions rather than leaving it empty benefits the property. Temperatures in closed up houses in coastal areas can get up to 150 degrees. Even wood furniture warps.

Like cars, properties do better when run a little. Without a tenant, someone will have to check the place, keep it aired out and free of mildew and provide the presence necessary to discourage vandalism, even squatting. These are reasons why many places also have housesitters.

Two types of renters

Native renters

The tenant-side of the rental market is made up of both working native Mexicans or North Americans who may be working, but likely are older.

Mexicans, of course, look for long-term rentals for the same reason we do in the U.S. They work in the city and need a place to live. They are moving a shorter distance within their own country so it is just a matter of moving from one place to another, bringing with them their refrigerators, ovens and light fixtures if need be. They will be signing a longer lease because longer leases give them more legal protection.

North American renters

You as a North American are renting to see what it would be like to live in Mexico and test the lifestyle, usually for a year or less. You should have little more than a few suitcases if you flew in and probably no more than a car load of personal items if you drove.

As a stranger in a strange land, you are very unlikely to not pay the rent, destroy a place, or squat. You don't have the same protections, cultural and legal, of a Mexican. These factors all come into play in the owner's decision-making, often making expats more desirable as tenants.

Rental agreements in Mexico favor renters. It is very difficult to evict a tenant in Mexico who has a lease of less than in two years, a potential risk factor that an owner can avoid by having a North American tenant. Many Mexican property owners will not rent their place out until they find one.

Cultural differences that give you leverage as a potential renter

Mexicans are warm and social. They don't leave anyone out. Families spend more time together. It's one of the qualities I love about the country. When I open my door to guests, I never know for sure how many people will be standing at the threshold. As a single person especially, I love that and wish my own country was the same way.

The condominium resort that I currently live in has both permanent residents (usually North American) and Mexican vacation renters. When visiting the pool area, both types of residents are enjoying the pool and adjoining restaurant and dining area. Whereas the foreign residents may be in groups of two to four people, the Mexican groups are likely *at least* six people.

Mexican culture is group culture. They draw their personal circle of space around the group, not around the individual, like Anglo-Saxons do. While culturally this is a lovely thing, for a homeowner renting out their property, it's more problematic. You would no more tell Mexican tenants how many guests they can have than you would try to tell them the number of friends and family members they can have.

Many American/Canadian rental owners have a restriction of "no guests," meaning that if they have agreed to rent the place to one or two people, that is how many people will be staying there.

To say "no guests," would be risible to say to a Mexican tenant (and to be honest, it offends me a little too).They know Mexicans would completely ignore such an obnoxious rule. Therefore North Americans who rent out their vacation homes often only rent to their countrymen, who generally arrive in isolated, lonely little sets of ones and twos.

But here's where it gets weird. Many Mexican owners will not rent to Mexicans either, especially in higher-end places. Mexico does not have housing discrimination laws and owners have a strong preference for North American tenants. I'm not saying it's fair, just that it is.

My Mexican friends who have spent a great deal of time in the U.S. admit to me that their fellow countrymen are less "cuidadosa" of personal property. As an American who rents out my own vacation condo in West Virginia with my own stories to tell about my countrymen as renters, I would be the first to argue against this bias, but I can't make it go away.

Whether the owner is Mexican or North American, these concerns make you a more desirable prospect as a renter and can give you substantial leverage. Many potential renters walk into a situation not realizing their negotiation power if they are North American, especially if they are willing to rent for a few months of low or a less popular season.

<u>First impressions count.</u> People can decide whether to rent to you based strictly on if they like you. Go into any such meeting as if it were a job interview.

When you have learned about new places to rent through your own networking and have found a way to get a letter/email to the owner of the property, you can make a request for consideration directly to them.

Below is a copy of one of mine, in both Spanish and English, since some of the owners are Mexican. You can it revise according to your own circumstances, seasons and conditions.

Petición

Estimado vecino,
Dear Neighbor,

Me gustaria presentarme, me llamo Kerry Baker. Llevo dos años alquilando un piso en este complejo turistico, la mayoria de de los meses de temporada baja. Normalmente alquilo entre Junio hasta Diciembre, más o menos.

I would like to introduce myself. My name is Kerry Baker. I have been renting an apartment in this resort for most of the low season. Normally I rent in Mexico between the months of June and December, more or less.

¡Me encanta esta edifico y su ubicación, qúe suerte tenga usted un piso aqui, el personal es estupendo!

I love this building and its location. How lucky you are to have an apartment here. The staff is wonderful!

Soy escritora. Trabajo sola en mi apartamento a diario, por eso aprecio mucho la energia de las personas que vienen y van. He rentado en otros lugares como en el norte o cerca del centro en el verano y estan demasiado tranquilos. Además aquí puedo tomar un autobus facílmente a mi gimnasio, donde voy la mayorla de los dias.

I am a writer. I work alone in my apartment every day and for that reason, really appreciate the energy of the people coming and going instead of the total quiet of other places I have rented up north in the summer. Moreover, from this resort, I can easily take a bus to my gym, which I do most days.

Quisiera yo pedir su consideración de esta petición mia alquilar su apartamento algun verano en el futuro, quizas el año que viene, en el caso que este apartamento que he alquilado los últimos dos años no este disponible.

I would like to ask your consideration of this request to rent your apartment for some summer in the future, even next year perhaps, in the case that the apartment that I have rented the last two years is not available.

Nunca se sabe la agenda de un dueño(a) y siempre sea posible que el piso se vaya a estar comprometido a sus amigas o familia durante ese plazo. No quiero depender demasiado en la disponibilidad de este piso.

You never know owners' schedules. It is always possible that the apartment will be promised to friends or family during this period. I don't want to depend too much on the availability of a single apartment and wanted to reach out to you.

Busco un contracto de seis meses, como es mucho mas dificIl encontrar un piso a un precio razonable durante un mes individual, particularmente en los meses de noviembre o tal vez diciembre, ya sabe usted.

I look for a commitment of six months because it's so difficult to find an apartment at a reasonable price for a single month, particularly in November and December as I'm sure you already know.

Como he mencionado, soy escritora, con una vida muy tranquil. No salgo mucho, no tengo mascotes y estoy muy cuidosa de mis alojamientos. Siempre dejo un apartamento un poquito mejor que se me encontro cuando salgo a regresar a Los Estados Unidos.

As I have mentioned, I am a writer, with a very quiet life. I don't go out much, nor do I have pets. I am very respectful of the properties I rent. I always leave an apartment a tiny bit better than I find it when I leave to return to the United States.

Lo más importante es que comprendo bien como cobran la electricidad durante esos meses. Estoy muy cuidadosa en mi utilización del aire. Sé que solamente se use en la habitación donde esté. Normalmente no lo uso mientras estoy concinando y sigo otros buenos hábitos conservadores despues de haber vivido aquí cuatro veranos.

But most important is that I understand very well how electricity is billed in Mexico during these months. I am very careful in my utilization of air conditioning. I know to only use it in the room I'm working in. Normally I don't use it when I cook and I have other good conservation habits having lived in the city for four summers now.

He adjuntado las facturas para tres de los cuatro meses que pasé aqui este año (la primera, lo más bajo, me quedé solamente tres semanas). Salí antes de llegar mi úlitima factura, pero puede preguntar en la oficina para examinarla. La agente de bienes raízes me pidió pagar lo mismo del mes anterior antes de irme a Guadalajara.

I have attached the bills for three of the four months that I spent here this year (the first, the lowest, I only stayed three weeks). I left before the final bill arrived but you can ask the office to permit you to see it. The real estate agent asked me to pay the same amount as the month prior before I left for Guadalajara to settle the account.

En el pasado, he pagado $850 dolares (15,300 pesos) por cada mes en la temporado baja y siempre pago la factura electrica también. Tal vez pueda pagar hasta $950 dolares (17,000 pesos), depende en lo que ofrezca el piso. Puedo pagar $1,100 dolares (20,000 pesos) por los meses de temporada alta de Noviembre y Deciembre.

In the past, I have paid $850 a month (15,300 pesos) for each month of low season and always pay the electric blll. I perhaps could go up to $950 dollars (17,000) depending on what the flat has to offer. I can pay up to $1,100 dollars a month (20,000 pesos) for the high season months of November and December.

También tengo muchas referencias locales, incluso de quienes aquilé por unos años antes, en Tierra Sands Condominios en el norte cerca de Marina El Cid..

I have many local references, including those from prior years, when I rented at Tierra Sands, which are condominiums near El Cid Marina.

Si usted necesita visitar durante este plazo por una o dos semanas, también podria yo visitar unas amigas que tengo en Guadalajara.

Because I have friends in Guadalajara that I like to visit once in a while, it would also be possible to visit them for a week or two if you need to visit your property once during this period.

Que hablo español pueda ser un benefico también en caso de que usted necesite algo hecho aqui, podria ayudarlo con cualquier tarea que sube. Prefiero tener ese tipo de amnistad con usted.

Since I speak Spanish, it might be a benefit to you as well in case you need something done here. I could help you with whatever task unexpectedly arises. I prefer to have that kind of relationship with you.

Si tiene usted algun interes en mi proposito, comuniquese conmigo al siguiente correo electronico kerryinmexico@gmail.com.

If you have an interest in my proposal, please communicate with me by email at Kerryinmexico@gmail.com

Muchas gracias por su atención y consideración!

Thank you so much for your attention and consideration!

Kerry Baker

Chapter Twelve

If a rental is up for sale

Sometimes a very good rental deal can be made when a property is up for sale. In this case, you will need to determine if you'd be willing to allow agents to show the property while you are living there. This has the potential of being inconvenient depending on the desirability of the house and how hot the market is.

If you are not present when the property is shown, your personal belongings may not be secure. Once, when I was renting my very first place, only for a month, I walked in to find the owner and a family in my apartment. The owner was showing it to future prospective tenants without my permission to enter. I raised hell. Assess the possibility of that happening and have those conversations if your owner or manager; especially in a B&B type situation.

The prospect of an occasional visit (with proper notice) might be of little inconvenience. You won't have many belongings there and will likely have a maid so you won't have to worry about cleaning up the place for a realtor to show it.

Terms requiring your presence during a showing or prohibiting entry need to be written into the contract and notarized for longer term stays. But seriously, a person's character is far more important than contracts in Mexico. Every place you rent should have a way to lock things up.

Chapter Thirteen

Getting Leads on Places

<u>In person - always the most effective</u>
Making contacts in a new town who can give you leads on places is a capricious process.

My first contact was literally a friend-of-a-friend-of-a-friend who knew someone in Mazatlán. A girlfriend of mine who is master networker took it as a personal challenge to find me a contact and delivered in less than a week. I met her contact (they'd never met) the first few weeks in Mexico and we are still good friends today.

For you, it could be a conversation at a coffee shop or reading something written online that makes you think you might like to get to know that person. Expats stand out. Talk to *everybody*. We expats can be a pretty scruffy lot. Don't let appearances deceive you or discourage you from reaching out.

Social Media
All popular areas in Mexico have either active Facebook pages or Yahoo groups. MySpace also has a very active website in Mexico. When you return from your one-month stay, start inquiring about longer-term rentals in your chosen town. You should be able to ferret out the good from the bad opportunities if you've taken good notes in your one-month stay. Ask people about specific complexes and neighborhoods you like.

Forums

Forums tend to draw the same 15 - 20 people responding all the time. They are still good sources of general information though, and worth an evening to read- through, especially when they discuss unscrupulous realtors to avoid and which ones they like and trust. I found the realtors I've used in Mexico after several people spoke highly of them on a forum.

The forums to start with are Expatforum.com, ExpatFocus.com and ExpatExchange.com, Expats.com, and Easyexpat.com. Don't forget to check the dates of the postings.

Local English online newspapers

Online and regular English language newspapers often have classifieds and forums. I met my current business partner when she ran an ad for a housemate in a local online newspaper. Local English or bilingual newspapers often have profile stories on expats. If someone sounds like a nice person, call and let him/her know how interesting you thought the story was. Expats usually are very welcoming of their brethren.

Spanish practice groups in your home town

Unless you already speak Spanish, you should be attending Spanish practice groups in the U.S if you live in a town sizable enough to host them. These groups attract people who have lived in Spanish-speaking countries, snowbirds with homes there. and travelers. Check Meetup.com for a listing of practice groups in your area.

Start talking about Mexico in all your social groups. I made one of my first key contacts in Mazatlán through a hiking group in Denver. She and her husband have a home there. Now we get to be friends in both cities.

Chapter Fourteen

Renting from snowbirds - some of your best opportunities

Many people can't help themselves. American cultural mores regarding homeowner-ship are firmly ingrained. Many people who love Mexico don't want to even spend part of their year there without owning their own home, regardless of the costs of upkeep and the risks of ownership. They cannot feel *at home* unless it's *their* home.

In every desirable Mexican town, many expats own lovely second homes and flats that they might be willing to rent out for months at a time if the *right* person (you) comes along. With so many people retiring to Mexico, recently named by *Forbes Magazine* as the best foreign retirement destination for U.S. citizens, the number of second homes in Mexico is likely to go up as well.

Income to these homeowners is generally somewhat secondary to care, upkeep, and trust because they have so little recourse should something go wrong. Many would favorably consider one conscientious person or couple paying $900 a month for six months ($5,400) over the prospect of to a series of groups of unseen strangers paying $2,000 for three months ($6,000) only for the high season.

The owners weigh the difference in income against wear and tear, cleanings, coor-dination, and security issues and often decide the peace of mind of one tenant or a couple they can trust is a better option.

Another optimal arrangement for an owner would be to split the timeframes to get top dollar for the most peak months while arranging long-term rentals that include still-pleasant shoulder months. Whenever considering a property, try to think how your offer would benefit the owner. Frame the conversation to their advantage.

Many high-profile places are not advertised

Many of the best places in the price range we are discussing ($600-1,500) are not advertised. The homeowner goes through social networks to locate tenants and then hires a property manager to only handle coordinating cleanings, airings, and check-in/outs.

If they do hire a realtor, that representative will not advertise the place either but instead will cautiously keep their eyes open for specific people calling in whom their homeowner/client would comfortable with. They will vet the prospect before presenting the unadvertised option. Again, this has to do with fewer legal protections and the complications of enforcing contracts in Mexico.

There are other reasons not to advertise a rental. Homeowner association agreements in upscale complexes may prohibit short-term rentals. Receiving income from a rental is complicated by the fear of being taxed by both countries. For these reasons the rental arrangement often is a private matter rather than a commercial one.

No one can prohibit an owner from having a friend stay in their apartment or home. Since the arrangement is based on a relationship, the owner will be seeking to determine if you will fit in with the people culture of the building or neighborhood. Are you a partier? Are you discreet?

When I moved to Denver, I lived with my uncle for two years. I paid him rent the same way I would any friend or family member with whom I lived with for over a month. When I was younger and lived in San Diego, I once moved into friends' place on the beach for almost a year (for which I paid $1,000 a month) when they had to work in another city because didn't want to lose their oceanfront lease. These informal arrangements are even more common within close-knit expat communities.

Your lodging relationship with this type of snowbird owner is often the same - a personal, private relationship and an agreement among friends.

Their property is more than a rental and you are more than a tenant

For a snowbird or second-home owner, the purpose of having a vacation home is to go for a month or two of vacation at a time and upon return, have the place be exactly as you left it, everything in place and working properly.

As a prospective tenant, they will be looking for signs that you will take care of the place as you would if you were a guest in the home of a good friend's *parents*, replacing things in-kind and watching over it as if it were your own.

Be discreet with others as to the nature of your arrangement

Expat communities are nosy and gossipy. People's barriers come down a little when they are in Mexico, which is part of the attraction. Sometimes snowbirds who rent their homes out feel awkward telling you directly not to discuss your rental arrangement with neighbors, even if they are "friends" of theirs. You have nothing to gain by sharing the details and may put the owner in an awkward position in the future.

Play it safe. Do not discuss your rent or even your relationship. Switch the topic to where to find the best shrimp *molcajete*.

The same awareness should extend to building staff. English-speaking personnel who work as security and maintenance in buildings with many expat homeowners move from property to property. Maintaining your reputation as "cuidadosa," responsible, friendly, respectful of Mexicans and sober most-of-the-time will be critical to maintaining your flow of housing opportunities.

Staying in second homes affordably: A cross between renting and house-sitting

This networking method of finding and securing long term stays in oceanfront or upscale properties in the range of $800 - $1,100 a month in vacation or second homes is a bit of cross between house-sitting and renting.

Like house-sitting

- You are staying off-season (or at least part of it)
- You are treating the property as you would if you were a guest in someone's

home, including replacements and repairs if necessary (Wouldn't you do that anyway?)

- You are staying in a beautiful home that you could not afford as strictly a snowbird

<u>Not like house sitting</u>

- You will have a few months of good weather, high season or shoulder months
- You are paying rent, therefore you have certain privileges and rights
- You can leave town if the opportunity arises and don't have house-sitters' responsibilities like taking care of pets
- Socially, you are viewed differently

<u>As a renter, be the person they want back</u>

One of the best things about living in Mexico is that once you develop a network and reputation, you can live in beautiful houses and apartments at far less than in the U.S. You can do a number of things to ensure you can choose from the best, especially when renting from North Americans with second homes.

If you are renting a second or vacation home, the owners is betting on you to leave less wear and tear over the course of your longer-term stay than groups of vacationers will leave over a series of shorter stays. They might even be generating less income renting to you than vacationers and are willing to trade some income for a tenant they can trust.

To return the favor, treat any second home as you would your own.

<u>Absolutely replace anything broken with the same quality item you broke</u> (I have a special skill with blenders myself. I learned they don't do well with Nutella.)

<u>Don't be petty about small things</u> Services in Mexico are much less expensive than in the U.S. Have the dirty rug shampooed if it needs it, or a blind replaced if it's broken. A typical service call of this kind in Mexico usually costs less than $20.

Be flexible with visits within the bounds of safety. If an owner unexpectedly needs to visit for a few days (sometimes things like Visa issues come up), be accommodating if you know them well enough and feel comfortable with their staying.

Communicate - If you have a problem, try to handle it yourself if possible, then communicate with the landlord or property management company and let them know what happened.

Write a thank you note at the end of your stay letting them know what you enjoyed the most about the place.

Consider leaving a small a gift or some type of small improvement (make sure they know it's from you and not the realtor or property management company). I have framed family pictures left on refrigerators and once replaced a lampshade. I was invited back for the next year before I even left the country.

If you are renting through a realtor or property manager, try to get the name of the owner. Understandably, realtors/property managers resist this because they're afraid you'll contact the owner directly the following year to rent the place on your own and they'll be out a commission.

Respect this relationship. The realtor worked hard for it. Still, try to get the owner's name. You might want them as a reference in the future, which is something harder to get from realtors and property managers who work with dozens of clients a year.

Remember the big picture - Expats are tight communities. They know one another and talk a lot. Be a good tenant/friend. The word will get out and you will never lack for options.

Know your limits of luxury - You may think this a really odd thing to include: Know your limit on how elegant a place should be for your particular lifestyle. High-end places sometimes come with sophisticated electronics and fragile objects d'art. Will you want to entertain? If something got broken, could you replace it?

Some guests, particularly Mexican guests, tend to bring their children with them on social calls more than we do. Can you take responsibility for them? As tempting as some places are, consider repercussions in terms of money and reputation if something went wrong.

If you only plan to have sober adult expats over, then you probably have nothing to worry about. If your guests are a bit more diverse, factor that into your rental choices.

Chapter Fifteen

Housesitting

Many people hire house sitters in Mexico when they go back north or are traveling. In return for staying free, house-sitters coordinate maids, gardeners, plumbers and other help. Often they also take care of a pet or two.

In Mexico, it's not a good idea to leave a place vacant for over a few weeks. Owners need to at least have someone be seen coming and going, collecting mail - a presence. This makes housesitting gigs off-season plentiful in many popular expat destinations.

For a person on a pension or a couple trying to get to know an area, this can be a lovely way to learn about Mexico and live well. I know several older single women who do this every year in Mazatlán. A good website is Housesitmexico.com. The company charges a membership fee. Alex, the owner, is well-loved by expats who finally get to leave town and their pets for a few months while they travel around Mexico.

One downside of house-sitting is that your stay might be strictly limited to the off-season, sometimes a very different experience to high season, which you probably would like to experience at least a bit of if you're thinking of ever living there permanently.

The other downside is that you are tied down. If an opportunity comes up for travel, you won't be able to go, especially if the deal includes care of pets.

Understanding how electricity is billed is particularly important if you are considering a house-sitting gig in Mexico in a coastal area or hot time of year. You need to know how much much electricity will you need to make the place habitable during the hot months (the times they most likely need house-sitters).

In the wrong house, without proper knowledge of how electricity is billed in Mexico, you may end up paying as much in electricity bills as you would renting a place on your own.

In coastal towns and hot areas, the government subsidizes electricity during the summer, but you still have to be very conservative, air-conditioning only the room you are in.
If electricity use goes over a certain red zone, the owner will be heavily penalized. People used to central air often have a hard time adapting or simply don't realize just how careful you have to be.

If the owner doesn't have past electric bills for those months to show you, you should be very cautious about a housesitting deal. In the wrong house you could end up with $500 a month electric/internet bill to survive in the heat while still being tied down to a pet and maintaining a house. Not worth it.

Chapter Sixteen

Keep cultivating leads

Even after you've found your ideal first place and settle in, keep looking. The first place is never the best place. Even if you love it, better places probably exist at a better price. You'll want to learn where they are for subsequent years.

It's easy to get swept up in the romance of it all. The chances that you negotiated the best deal for the best location the first time out of the gate in a new town in another country is virtually nil.

Every year I think I've found the best place, and every subsequent year I've found one even better. Every place will have it's pros and cons. By renting a different place each time, optimally for at least six months at a time, you learn what you can live with and without. The answers will surprise you.

As you are out meeting people, especially expats, you may hear someone talking about a condo available or a home that snowbird lives in very part-time Call and introduce yourself or ask to be introduced by a mutual acquaintance.

Tell them that although you are very happy where you are, you visit every year and always like to meet your fellow expats. Invite them to breakfast and get to know them. Try to work what type of arrangement they might be looking if they were ever to rent the place into the conversation and keep the information for subsequent years.

Every season you spend in your prospective new Mexican home town, you should be taking notes of other upscale buildings or neighborhoods you like. When they come up in conversations and leads, you'll want to know which is which.

This year I stayed in a beautiful three bedroom ocean view condo that I heard about two years ago after I committed to another place. Even though I was living across town at the time I took a picture of the building for future reference.

When the owners unexpectedly e-mailed me the following year while I was in the U.S to see if I would be interested, I could retrieve what it looked like. Later I rented their place during a high-season month for $450.

More than tenants and landlords, we are fellow-expats and as such are part of a network that helps us navigate the various differences in the way things operate in Mexico.

When you see a place for rent that you like, even if it's out of your price range, get information, particularly if the condo is new.

What I have found is that after a few years of dealing with the comings and goings of large groups of people on vacation tearing up things they have so carefully chosen for the home, owners sometimes begin to favorably consider a nice quiet single person or couple for a longer term rental, even at a reduced rent.

When you find your first great place, check out other apartments in the same building you are in. Again, being there off-season is a huge advantage. People aren't in them. You're kind of special, almost a local. In the lazy days of summer when you're hanging out, many on-site property managers will be willing to show you other apartments that occasionally rent out under the radar.

If you see something you'd like in some future date or year, tell the on-site manager and make a note of it. Sometimes building on-site staff can put you directly in touch with the owner without anyone having to cover a realtor's commission. If you like the building, it doesn't hurt to ask.

Be aware that within the same buildings you rent you will find a big range of difference in livability in the units. Don't assume because your flat is fantastic that the one on the opposite corner of the building with an identical floor plan will be too. My current building boasts both gorgeous condos (which I create index files on) and ones I wouldn't stay in for single week-end.

Covering gaps in your stays

Sometimes availability of a place may fall short of a month or two of your time frame. For example, you have secured a dream place but want to arrive in July and it's not available until August.

By having developed relationships, you can often find places to fill in the gaps if you are waiting for a place to open up or if your contract/agreement ends a month or so before you want to leave the country.

Another situation might be that you have a six- month lease - minus one month. For example, a situation such as someone being able to rent it to you at a greatly reduced rate from July to February, except for the month November, which was committed to someone two years ago.

In a situation like this, if you have kept cultivating relationships, you may be able to propose an AirBnB type situation with another snowbird if the month falls in during high-season. Sharing a house for such a limited time can be an easy, even enjoyable solution.

Especially if you're single, it's nice to have company now and then in a foreign country. Invariably, in those instances, you exchange information about living in your host country that you wouldn't have found out otherwise.

The period of transition of moving to a new country is no time to be a recluse. You will need a great deal of information to make your new life remarkable *and* inexpensive.

Even if by nature you aren't very outgoing, you will need to buck up for several years in order to learn about how to live in your new country and develop the necessary social support system. Networking for the best housing available facilitates friendships.

Chapter Seventeen

Reputation counts, theirs and yours

The first step to paying $700 to $1,100 a month for a well-appointed two bedroom oceanfront or high-end condominium/home or an upscale "El Centro" area for 6-10 months in Mexico is understanding how much you, as a North American are preferred as a tenant and then honing that competitive edge with references, discretion and a demonstrated respect for property. The second is be willing to incorporate a few off-season months into your long-term stay (I guess that was actually a bunch of steps).

People will be watching you. I recently was invited to rent a high-rise luxury apartment that goes for $3,500 a month during high season (In the spirit of full-disclosure, the lowest rent I could negotiate was $1,500, out of my price range). It looked like Robert DeNiro's oceanfront place in the fabulous movie "Heat." The entire ocean-facing wall was a window with panoramic view of the Pacific from the seventeenth floor. The elevator served only two apartments. Unlike DeNiro's place, it had furniture.

Unbeknownst to me, every prior time I'd visited the building, neighbors were evaluating me and reporting to the person unofficially acting as a rental agent on whether they thought I'd fit in.

One of Mexican staff members had worked at a previous place I'd lived. He had been the night concierge there. He knew my nocturnal habits (We had shared some fascinating late-night conversations about the supernatural) and the type of guests I had. Like many personnel in expat communities, his English was excellent and he could tell owners practically anything they wanted to know about me if asked. Expats are a tight group and word travels fast, good and bad.

Chapter Eighteen

Rental concierges: Pay someone to look at your final choices before you commit if you can't be there yourself.

Hopefully, after your first month, you have gone back home and done your research. By now you have narrowed your selection to 2-3 places you've found listed online or through realtors online.

If you don't have a local friend to look at it in person for you, you will need to hire a third party to look at your prospective place or places to make sure they were honestly represented online or by the realtor.

I have included a list of rental concierges in this book. These are people with an online presence who you can contact about reviewing your place for you. A checklist is provided in this book to give you a start on questions they should ask for you. I do not receive any remuneration other than the cost of this book for the listing, so no other costs will be built into their fee.

A rental concierge can test all systems (air conditioner, internet, water, toilets, appliances, security) and get an impression of the other side, the owner or realtor.

The extra step of hiring a rental concierge, along with having had researched the names of reputable (and disreputable) agents in forums before selecting your final choices should give you peace of mind.

There is a big difference between living in a place for a few weeks of vacation (when you are out all the time anyway) and living in a place for six months or more, including some hot or rainy low season months when you'll want to be inside. Do not let saving a hundred dollars or so prevent you from carrying out this critical step of seeing the place before you sign on.

If you get one thing out of this booklet, take this advice. I can't stress it enough. Photos can be deceiving. They can't convey noise level and they can't inventory the cookware you'll need for a six-month-plus stay. Photos can't test the air conditioning or the internet.

Pay an independent outside party to personally visit the unit for you and take their own pictures. Photos are good. Videos are better. Pictures can make units look much bigger than they are. I've seen properties advertised as penthouses with wrought-iron *interior* furniture and one lamp per room. You know what that means: Spring Break.

If at all possible, ask that the place be checked out at night. Some neighborhoods are quite noisy - dogs barking, music, roosters. The time to know the real character of an area is at night.

What properties surround it? Is there an empty building right behind it that encourages crime? Is there a mildew smell from the place not being aired out properly in previous summers?

If you intend on coming back and forth a lot, a professional relationship with a concierge or a local expat with good sense and knowledge of the area can be invaluable. Some concierges can stock your fridge, pick you up from the airport and warn you of places to avoid. They often know the local gossip.

Experienced part-time expats even keep property managers on a modest retainer at times to ensure that their calls are always answered first. The rental concierges listed in the book have a range of backgrounds that might enable them to meet other needs you might have in the future.

Expect to pay concierges fairly, anywhere from $50 (dollars) for a single simple task taking under an hour to $100 or more if including travel time. This might be the most important relationship you have in Mexico in the first few years. It was mine, and the fees was more than worth it.

Please, don't take advantage of rental concierges for free errands that you think shouldn't be a big deal (I heard this as a chief complaint of my business partner, also a property manager and concierge). Time is time, regardless of how "easy" a task is.

Once you've narrowed it down to your top 2-3 rental choices, set your rental concierge loose to set up appointments with the owner or their representative to check them out on your behalf.

Do not allow yourself to be pressured by any realtor or owner into accepting a place without the step of either seeing the place yourself (perhaps during your first one-month visit) or setting up a concierge to see it for you.

While it may be possible for a concierge to be fooled, if they were, console yourself that you most assuredly would have been fooled as well. Noise is the easiest thing to miss. Last summer, in spite of hiring my concierge to check the place out, I found that mariachi bands played downstairs at the hotel next door some Saturday and holiday evenings, something impossible for her to have known. Otherwise, the place was a dream come true and still one of my favorites.

No place will be perfect. You will need to make choices. You will have to decide things like whether the noise level is worth being at the heart of the action, whether the exterior of the building is important, or whether you are willing to go out and buy necessary cookware (Bring "unusual" cooking utensils you use and less common spices with you). However, a rental concierge can prevent many a disaster.

Chapter Nineteen

Checklists for renting

These are some of the things that you will want to make sure to ask the realtor or owner about on any property you are considering. To whatever extent possible, verify the information through your rental concierge.

<u>Questions you need to ask, then need to be confirmed on-site by your concierge;</u>

- What is the gas situation for cooking and heating? Is it already hooked up, or do you need to do it? Is there a gas cylinder or do you need to contract this yourself? If so what is the deposit on the tank?
- Is there an alarm system?
- Are there any tools available; anything from plungers to brooms.
- If you watch television, what television service is provided? Do you have to set it up yourself? Cable or satellite TV service in Mexico is quite good. Sky TV is a Mexican service with some English-speaking channels. The most popular TV services are Dish Network (American) and Shaw Direct (Canada) which includes NBC, CBS, ABC, and PBS.
- Is water filtered or delivered? What is the process? Even when water is filtered, I am hesitant to drink it from the tap. If it is delivered, who pays and how much does it cost?
- How is the water bill paid? Is there a meter or is the fee set?
- If located inside a Fraccionamiento (Development) find out who pays any dues.
- What do I do if there's no internet? (not just "Is there internet?" Try to test it as speed and reliability vary quite a bit even from building to building.
- Telephone service (check that there is no outstanding debt)

- Air conditioning functioning
- Extra sheets/bedding including a blanket
- Where do I park my car?
- If you have a pet, are they permitted? (Most Mexican homes have tile floors, making it easy to clean up after a pet. You may be able to negotiate this.)
- What exactly is the public transportation system?.
- If you want to hail a cab, will you need to call by telephone or will you be able to hail them from the street (important in negotiating fare)
- Is housekeeping included? How is that coordinated?
- What is the state of the shower?
- How often is the place fumigated? What if I need one? (A biggie in coastal areas where the "bichos" (bugs) seem big enough to steal your car.)
- What about a washer/dryer or laundry service?
- Neighbors / Noise level
- Does it have an oven? A surprising number of places don't, and it's easy to miss.
- Security - good locks and building security or a gated community with a "vigilante" on guard

Make sure there's no balance on the electric or telephone bill when you take the place and know exactly what to expect in terms of the bill.

<u>Kitchen Checklist:</u>

Is there an oven? Believe it or not, it's easy to miss that you don't have one. You see a stovetop and assume an oven is below it. Many rentals don't have them at all, which can be a problem for a long term stay unless they've installed a good system of toaster ovens, microwaves and plenty of stovetop burners.

I was surprised to learn that ovens are the bane of existence for Mexicans as well as expats. Often they are gas, which many of us are no longer used to anymore. The dials may be in Spanish and/or rubbed out with no precise temperature dial and lighting them can be fraught with anxiety. Get a good orientation from your realtor on how to operate the oven and any appliances like washers and dryers as the written instructions are probably in Spanish.

Suggested Cookware:

- Three skillets, two large, one small
- Medium and small saucepans
- A larger caldron with two handles
- Coffee cups
- Dish towels/ oven mitts
- Coffee-maker
- Set of small/medium/large bowels
- Pasta Strainer
- Microwave and microwave-safe containers
- Oven or larger toaster oven
- A Stovetop with at least two burners
- 6 dinner plates, six small plates
- 4-6 dinner bowls
- Small/medium/large mixing bowls
- Silverware
- tongs/spatulas/wooden spoons
- Toaster oven pans if toaster oven is used
- Baking pans and baking sheet, small and large if you have an oven
- Sets of large and small glasses
- Ice cube trays
- Dish soap
- Large spoons
- Peeler
- Wine opener
- blender
- Set of good knives
- Cutting boards
- Wine glasses
- Can opener
- Crockpots (optional but great to have in hot summers or if you don't have an oven)
- Gas oven igniter, they look like a cigarette lighter but with a longer extension, should be provided.

<u>Pictures/videos for the concierge to take:</u>
- View
- Yards
- Entrance
- Neighborhood
- Kitchen
- Bathroom - check faucets and showers and under the basin for cleanliness and plumbing leaks.

Finally, how does the place smell? Even high-end places can develop a mildew smell if the landlord has cut corners on maintenance in the past. Places in coastal and rainy areas should be aired out at least twice a month in low season.

Sometimes owners who have not been there off-season don't believe that. Ultimately they pay a bigger price because the smell is almost impossible to get rid of once it's taken hold. Maybe the smell won't bother you over time. Maybe it will decrease with airings. Maybe it's a deal breaker.

<u>Consider making minor improvements if staying six months or more</u>

Flats and houses are rented out "as is." If a place is perfect but needs a minor improvement, you might consider paying for it when you get to Mexico, with the permission of the owner.

While paying for an improvement on such a short-term rental would be unheard of at home, labor is very inexpensive in Mexico. I have paid for an additional lock on a bedroom door for $30. A "blockade bar," one that reaches across the entire front door, may cost less than $100 and may be worth the additional peace of mind. For an otherwise perfect place, it may be well-worth it.

If you have any concerns whatsoever about safety, either make a recommendation for the improvement or pass on the place.

<u>Electricity - Another key component in negotiating rent</u>

Unless you have a full-service rental in a resort area or are renting a vacation home, you will likely be responsible for paying all the utilities including water and gas as well as electricity.

It's important that you know how electricity is billed in Mexico in coastal and other hot areas before embarking on your negotiation in one of those areas. The cost of electricity in Mexico is one of the reasons so many luxury properties stand empty in low season.

If you are renting (or house sitting) totally or partially off-season in a coastal area when the weather is hot, you will be likely responsible for the electric bill. The owner will need to trust that you know how to conserve energy in a way you may not be used to in America where often we cool entire houses.

During the hottest months of summer until November 1, electricity is subsidized in Mexican coastal towns and other very hot areas. The rate/bill should be low if you adopt the same conservation habits as Mexicans do.

- Use the air conditioner only in the room you are in. Most apartments/condos have mini splits with remotes to turn off and on as you leave and enter the room.

- The biggest user of energy is the refrigerator so make sure you don't leave the door open, as you unpack groceries for example.

- Draw the blinds at the height of the day.

- Do not air condition the kitchen when you cook. Either buy a bathing suit and cook in the heat (use crock pots, make smoothies and salads rather than use the oven) or order take-out/delivery. It's almost as cheap to eat out as to cook your own meals in Mexico anyway. Get delivery food for several meals at a time (a delivery will cost you about $15, including delivery fee).

- Stick to air conditioning and working in the smaller room at the height of the day. Avoid trying to air condition a large, high-ceiling living room in mid-to-late afternoon.

- On November 1 the subsidy ends and electricity rates go up drastically. If you still need air conditioning from time to time, be particularly conservative and use fans or in the case of high-rises, use the ocean breezes. Using air conditioning only a few times when no subsidy is given will generate roughly the same bill as you will get in the hottest months if you follow conservation guidelines in this book. That's how huge a difference the subsidy makes.

In Mexico, if the electric bill goes over a certain level of usage, the owner will be penalized for months or even a year with much higher rates. Some owners are willing to let spectacular places stand empty in the summer in coastal areas rather than risk it,

Reassure any potential short-term landlord that you practice excellent conservation habits. Follow them or you will be in for a nasty surprise when the monthly bill comes.

Before renting, make sure that there is no outstanding balance on the electric bill. Ask questions about what past usage has been in the months that you are staying. You need to know that you can comfortably air condition at least one room of the house at all times and will be able to keep the electric bill down within your budget.

If you killed on negotiating the rent, you might be able to budget a bit more for air conditioning, but remember there is a "no fly zone" for usage. Once a consumer goes over a certain limit, the landlord is penalized heartily and mercilessly by the electric company for months, maybe even a year. You have to make sure that never happens to you or your owner.

Other utilities

Make sure there is no outstanding payment left by previous owners. Utility bills can be paid at a local convenience store or bank as long as they are not overdue, or the property manager will collect them.

Mexico does not have public gas service, so if your home needs gas, you will have to purchase it from a private company. Many houses have gas estacionario (stationary gas tanks) with a readable meter. You call the gas company and refill the tank when the gas runs low.

Telephone service is the most complicated and expensive utility. For that reason, many rental homes do not come with ground lines, and those that do may ask for an additional deposit (phone bills can run hundreds of dollars if international calls are made).

If your rental home doesn't have a phone, it may be possible to solicit a new line although I can't imagine doing so for a stay of less than a year.

Before you leave, check into international (Canada/U.S)/Mexico plans with your phone carrier. You will want to adjust your data and calling plan while you're gone and add free international calling. When you return home, you go back to the store and change the plan back to your original plan.

If you must, you need to visit Telmex to check availability and buy a new line in your name. Once you move out, you should cancel the associated address.

Chapter Twenty

Making the deal

Don't expect to get a beautiful place for $500 a month in any of the most popular expat areas. You should expect to pay at around $600 for places equitable to places you would rent in the U.S for $1,100 - $1,600 in medium-sized to larger cities in the U.S. (not including the most expensive cities in America; Boston, NYC, San Francisco for example).

Yes, you can find decent places to rent in Mexico for $500, but you will have to make a sacrifice in terms of the number of expats around, neighborhood safety, parking, interior and creature comforts (like air conditioning!).

If you're offering to pay rent for a high-end place during a month or two when it is unlikely an owner will be able to rent the unit (except to vacationers who are more likely to tear the place up), you should be in the position to work a great deal.

Regardless of what you are told or read online, there are no national standard practices for deposits or method of payment when you rent a place.

Those things depend on the judgment of the owner or realtor and the area. Whether the place you are considering is being rented through a realtor, property manager or owner, do not wait for them to give the price. Rental rates are often inflated if you are North American. Don't be afraid to tell them your budget and make an offer.

The biggest mistake I made in the first year when I was renting for my first five months was asking the question "How much is the rent?" Seems like a fair question, doesn't it? You ask it all the time in the U.S.

Always make an offer instead. Say, "I can pay X" or "My budget is X." Set budget parameters; the optimal and the most you will pay. Start as low as your conscience permits. My conscience level for an oceanview place begins at $800 a month, including at least one high season month. Leases in Mexico cannot legally extend beyond two years.

I would really think twice about paying over $1,000 a month during a city's low season regardless of its view unless I was allowed at least one high-season month at a greatly reduced rate.

For example, you might pay $850 a month for four months of the low season and a shoulder month in a coastal area and $1,100 for a high season month (when the rent might normally be $1,800 or more). Another combination could be $1,100 for the last month of the high season and $800 for each low-season month.

The issue is not strictly the rent but rather the most bang for the buck. Eight-fifty a month may sound pretty pricey for rent in Mexico, but not when it's a 2,000 square foot house facing the ocean or is in the center of town and has an interior pool and garden. Renting during the least popular times can help you lock in the good months too.

High and low seasons vary a little from city to city in Mexico but even in cities where the weather is practically always nice, snowbirds tend to favor certain months, leaving the other months loaded with opportunity.

Will your offer always work? No. You might run into a few owners who insist on the same high rates regardless of season or time. If property owners get lucky once or twice, they get overly confident that there will always inexperienced Americans or Canadians around to rent a place at an inflated rate.

Sometimes their logic (lack of) astounds me. I once tried to negotiate a two-bedroom oceanfront apartment I'd previously rented for $950 a month during mainly low season down to a more realistic $800 a month after having learned the market better. The owner turned me down.

His place stood empty for all but a few weeks of the six months plus had to be aired out and maintained weekly for a property management fee. I found a far superior place for $850 a month in a much better location. He was out over $5,000 between rent and property management fees, plus turning down a tenant who had an established history of leaving a place better than she found it. Some people, you have to accept, have more money than sense.

Keep places whose owners turn you down on file. Circle back in a few years if you need to. They might have come back to their senses.

Chapter Twenty-One

Agreements and Payments

<u>Deposits to reserving a place -</u> Ask that the amount required to reserve a place (maybe 20% of the rent amount) be applied against the first month's rent.

This book concentrates on rentals of less than one year. If you happen to want to brave a year-long rental, Mexican landlords will ask for a contract and they will have a notary public (which is Mexico's equivalent to a lawyer).

In the case of an actual lease, the notary will draft up the paperwork. The cost will be anywhere from MXP 900 to MXP 1,200 which you will pay. The only contract that counts is the one in Spanish so make sure it's translated by someone you trust. Read it carefully.

<u>Security deposits? Best to assume you are not getting that back</u>

If the landlord also asks for a security deposit, don't count on getting that deposit back, no matter how you baby the place.

I'm going on a bit of a cultural limb here, but I think these points are the most valuable in the book. I have put this issue to a number of Mexicans in the business of renting. They don't come out and say, "Of course the owners don't return your deposit money, you silly gringa," but they don't deny it either.

I have gone as far as run it by my Mexican friends in related businesses, people I know socially and trust. Even they seem a little fuzzy on the deposit concept, perhaps mentioning the latest Iphone that everyone in Mexico wants.

Personally, I would not expect to get a security deposit back even from a realtor because the actual owner could still be Mexican with that here foretold mentioned fuzzy understanding of deposits. You never really know the arrangement the owner and realtor have and where loyalties lie.

I am convinced the unwillingness to refund is not a character flaw or dishonesty, it's a cultural difference that affects Mexicans and tourists alike in purchasing almost anything.

Even in high-end retail stores, it's unlikely that you will get a cash refund for any item you purchase that doesn't work out. You may get credit, but no refund. Once money is received, that's who is keeping it. Assume that in any situation in Mexico and let any exception be a pleasant surprise. They really do not like giving money back.

Even rental sites run by North Americans have written on their website that a deposit is required even for shorter term rentals.

A damage deposit may be a reasonable request yet is not set in stone. If it's excessive and you are renting off-season you should have room to negotiate, perhaps by mentioning what you've paid in the past and providing references (which you'll have after the first year.)

Owners/property managers and even realtors from time to time play games like telling you that you have to pay 3-6 months rent in advance because you don't have a local guarantor, a co-signer. This is not a standard operating practice. Owners have come up with it because they think they can and/or have gotten away with it in the past.

Even if you get the deposit down to a more plausible amount, I'd think twice before renting from someone who would employ such tactics. Cheerfully decline. After all, Mexican renters generally don't provide co-signers and six-months advance rent. Neither should you.

You can expect this kind of opportunism when people can see you are under pressure. It's another reason why you should give yourself time, a month or more to find the right place, not a week-end. A small security deposit and first and last month's rent is the absolute most you should pay and try to negotiate that down as much as possible. You will have more leverage when they have choices.

If you do a significant deposit, in the last month of your rental period, instead of paying the full rent, tell them that you are making a partial payment and to use what you gave them as a deposit for the balance of that month's rent. That's what Mexicans do.

Get terms of stay in writing

You get things in writing not because realtors and property managers are untrustworthy, you get details in writing so you don't have misunderstandings about your length of stay, rent per month and your arrival and departure dates. Contracts at this level don't carry near the weight in Mexico that they do elsewhere. For that reason, character and reputation are much more crucial in all negotiations in Mexico.

You need to make clear to your realtor that any place you rent for six months or more must first be seen either by your or your rental concierge/representative. They may tell you that many people rent places sight unseen. Point out that you are not one of them. Again, starting your rental period in low season gives you more leverage.

Make sure your e-mails have detailed confirmations of your plans and agreement of payment amount month by month since it may vary from month to month depending on where in falls in high and low season.

Payments

With North American landlords, transferring the rent directly from your account into their account is a usual standard procedure. Now and then, owners prefer cash delivered to the property manager. Property managers sometimes pay bills and other maintenance expenses for the home owner, so the property manager might keep an account for them, deducting the expenses from the rent income.

Mexico is more of a cash-driven country, which is a little unnerving to those of us from a society where it's normal to leave the house with no more than a debit card and some change.

It's not that unusual for an owner to want the rent in cash, only annoying because it will require several trips to the A.T.M. each month, spaced 24 hours apart, to accumulate the cash for your monthly rent since A.T.M. withdrawals are limited to about 7,000 pesos and will not allow more than one withdrawal over a 24-hour period.

Realtor companies vary. Some take checks but not credit cards. Some will take your credit card and not cash. It's all over the board. If they take checks, make sure the check is accurate to the finest detail. Print out the parts not requiring cursive. Banks are incredibly picky about accuracy in Mexico - you can't just circle a mistake an initial it like in the U.S

Pagare Notes

With your contract, I understand sometimes you might be required to sign promissory notes or, in essence, an I.O.U. in advance of your payments. These are called "PAGARE" notes. Each one will be numbered and pre-dated for the dates your rent is due for however long you have signed a lease, i.e., six-month lease, six Pagare Notes.

Make certain you receive the dated and numbered note back each time you make a payment. This is your protection and proof of payment. Don't leave any payments for your landlord without receiving back your pre-dated Pagare Note.

Get Receipts

Be sure to get original receipts for each rent payment. Copies do not hold up in court. Nor do any contracts that are not in Spanish.

Receipts should state in detail what the funds are for, whether or not they are refundable and what conditions that must be met for a refund. There should also be a number of days before the refund is received by the payee if a refund is warranted, but don't say I didn't warn you about refunds.

Chapter Twenty-Two

Apartments are taken as is. Plan on paying for any minor repairs that come up.

Often in Mexico, the owner/landlord expects you to take care of problems that arise. If you have handyman skills that might not be a problem. Otherwise, you should ask around for the names of plumbers, electricians and others to have on hand. Don't take their word for it that any repairs will be made after you move in.

If you make any improvement, it should be the type that can be removed easily and taken with you to your next location or stored somewhere until you choose your next location. If you wish to paint any of the interior of your rental, get permission from the owner or property manager in writing before you change anything in the property.

If you cause any damage to the home, including appliances, you will be responsible for repairs. Many times, property owners have service contracts on their appliances. Check with the property owner to see if that's the case. If you have pets, make certain they are approved in your rental agreement.

If paying for repairs sounds scary, remember that repairs are usually very inexpensive in Mexico. A 30-minute visit from an electrician or plumber shouldn't cost over 300 pesos ($15). A $100 (U.S) repair would be a major one by Mexican standards. Mexicans can fix anything and they can fix it cheap. Don't even bother asking for the money from your landlord for the repair. They'll know you're a rookie.

To be on the safe side, expect this to be the norm whether the owner is North American or Mexican. North American owners sometimes take on the habits and customs of their host country, a "When in Rome," attitude.

Absolutely do not move into a house or condo if there is a repair or renovation you expect and need unless you are ready to pay for it.

If the condo is a part of a more upscale building where a monthly property management fee is being paid, a repair may be covered in that agreement. For example, my current rental is in a resort that also has privately owned condos. When a storm blew out two windows, the cost was covered by the unit owners' property management fees. Even if it hadn't been, the cost would have been a fraction of what the same damage would cost in the U.S.

Owner's responsibility on leased property for major repairs

If you find a house, condo or apartment to rent/lease, you must make certain the owner, landlord or property manager has the responsibility, in writing, for all and any structural, appliance and outdoor maintenance.

We have heard of experiences where owners expect the renter to repair roof leaks, etc. Those are not your responsibility. To be honest, I would not accept any place that was not move-in ready regardless of what the contract says.

Should something go awry, yes, you can go to a lawyer if you have a clear contract in Spanish. However, lawyers in Mexico are pretty toothless (notaries are the ones with status).

What lawyers can help with however is writing up in good Spanish any complaint you have for delivery to the PROFECO (Protection Federal of Consumers). Their services are inexpensive (that goes along with being powerless). A session should not run you more than 600 pesos.

When it comes to this type of issue PROFECO has more clout in Mexico than lawyers do.

<u>What if you don't like the furniture?</u>

Anything you rent for short-term will come furnished in Mexico. If you tell them that you don't like the furniture, they often will just move it into your spare bedroom. Not exactly what you had in mind, huh? Another reason to have a concierge who can take pictures.

I've never been able to find out why so few storage companies exist in Mexico.

Chapter Twenty-Three

Rent Increases

This book focuses on renting for less than a year. If you happen to rent a place for over a year (and have the proper visas), I have read that by law, landlords cannot raise the rent more than 10%. I have been unable to get this confirmed as a law throughout Mexico.

If your rent is raised by over 10%, go to the local office of the consumer affairs department, PROFECO (Procuraduría Federal de Consumidor) and find out. Some cities have a three-strikes-you're out policy, meaning if a landlord has three unresolved disputes, he can no longer rent out his property. If you have a problem, mention you will be visiting the consumer affairs office and see how your landlord reacts.

Chapter Twenty-Four

Your place is about so much more than renting at the best price

Think about past moves you have made. Didn't the first people you met in a new city (and the people you met through them) ultimately coalesce into your primary circle of friends? Don't underestimate the importance of your first year in Mexico in determining the tone of many years to come.

How you go about securing your first place shouldn't be seen in isolation, but rather as part of building a system that meets many different kinds of needs; the need for the right friends (expat and Mexican), the need for security and the need for a living space that inspires you - all while living within a budget.

Where you live always determines the type of people you meet and the tone of your subsequent social life. In Mexico, speaking some Spanish and developing Mexican friends will determine how integrated you feel and how much money you save. They can tell you what things should cost and can lead you to less expensive rentals over time.

Having an appealing place that you will want to share with them and others facilitates the development of these relationships. They are tied together.

It's not just a place. It's your springboard. Make sure it launches you in the direction of the life in Mexico you've been dreaming about.

Listing of Rental Concierges

Judy Dykstra
E-mail: Jubob2@hotmail.com
Jubob2 - Skype
Website/blog: judykystrabrown.com
387-761 0281
Chapala and surrounding areas

Daniella Barrera
Yucatan Concierge (yucatanconcierge.com)
52 1 552 559 8547
52 999 923 3597
Skype: yucatan.concierge
E-mail: daniela@yucatanconcierge.com
Serves the Yucatan Peninsula

Cesár Dorantes Benitez
residenciasuniversitariaslapaz@hotmail.com
E-mail: cdorant@itesm.mx
Skype: live:dorantescesar
Phone numbers: 045 222 505 1091
From Mexico: 222 505 1091
Serves Puebla

Indra Rojo Chapman
Indrarojo : INDRAROJOSKYPE
Indrarojo@yahoo.com
http://www.facebook.com/LoveCancun2010/
Serves the Yucatan Pennisula

Tina Marie Ernspiker
www.gringoslocos6.com
gringoslocos6@gmail.com
Facebook: https://www.facebook.com/gringoslocos6
Serves Morelia and Uruapan

Albania Kuri Hernandez
kuri.hdez@mextage.com
Associate: Bárbara Reyna Vazquez
E-mail: reyna.vazquez@mexstage
Mexstage (www.mexstage.com)
999 315 5772
Skype: Mexstage
Serves the Yucatan Peninsula

Christopher Kerr Hoffman
And mother, **Patty Hoffman**
Home phone +52(777)313_7331
Patty's Whatsapp +52(777)787_9256
Christopher's whatsapp +52(777)161-0373
Christopher's email: christopherkerr87@hotmail.com
E-mail: pattyaqui@yahoo.com.**mx**
Skype: pattyaqui
Serves Cuernavaca

Ana Paula Aguirre Hall
Email: aguirrehall@yahoo.com.**mx**
Cell: 777- 206 6655
Skype: ana.paula.aquirre
Serves Cuernavaca

Katie O'Grady
Blog: Los O'Gradys in Mexico
E-mail: losogradysinMexico@gmail.com
http://www.losogradysinmexico.com
Serves La Cruz de Huanacaxtle, Nayarit, Bahía de Banderas Jalisco/Nayarit area including Puerto Vallarta, La Cruz, Punta Mita, Sayulita and San Pancho.

José Santos
Josesantosfineart@gmail.com
0052 (951) 3314927
Serves Oaxaca

Adriana Torres Solis
Telephone: 044 415 103 9962
Email: adriana.toso9@gmail.com
Skype: aristoso9 / Aris Torres
Serves San Miguel de Allende

Audrey Zikmund
Lake Chapala
E-mail: az62343@gmail.com
Home: 376-106-0821
Cell: 331-862-7148
Serves Chapala and the surrounding areas

51888730R00085

Made in the USA
Lexington, KY
07 September 2019